Graphic Organizers Across the C...
Grade Three

D0690667

Table of Contents

Graphic Organizers Across the Curriculum
Grade Three

Introduction

Graphic organizers are tools for learning that allow students to see on paper what they may have trouble thinking through in their minds. Graphic organizers present a clear, visual picture of a concept or measurement that gives students a unique opportunity not only to grasp the concept presented, but also to move beyond it toward understanding related concepts. Graphic organizers help students to see relationships, to structure thinking, to remember vocabulary, facts, and concepts, and to acquire and apply their skills and knowledge. *Graphic Organizers Across the Curriculum* provides teachers with reproducible materials to help students gain this knowledge through interpreting, using, and creating a variety of graphic organizers.

Students' learning and teachers' effectiveness today are assessed through national standards. Standards across the curriculum require that students be able to read, interpret, and use graphic organizers of all kinds in every subject area. Students are often expected to interpret information in graphic organizers on standardized tests.

Organization

This book is organized into six units: Charts and Tables, Diagrams, Graphs, Lines, Maps, and Language and Memory Aids. Within each category are several kinds of graphic organizers. First, there is a blank graphic organizer that can be used to fit a variety of lesson plans. These blank organizers can be used with the activities in this book and with your own classroom activities. Then, there is a completed example of each graphic organizer. These examples are indicated by the icon ◐ in the upper right corner and are meant to give students a clearer picture of how the graphic organizer can be used. Finally, there are exercise pages, indicated by the icon ⚬, using the various graphic organizers. These lessons can be used to supplement your curriculum and give your students the opportunity to use and interpret graphic organizers.

The directions indicate which blank graphic organizer to reproduce and provide to students.

Icons representing curriculum areas are shown at the bottom right of each example and lesson page. These icons are also shown on the Correlation to Curriculum on page 5. The icons will assist in integrating these lessons into your lesson plans.

There is a Letter to Parents on page 6. Talk about the letter with your students, and send it home to enhance communication and understanding between parents and the school.

Use

The lessons in this book are meant to supplement your curriculum. It is assumed that the students will have some familiarity or prior instruction before completing these pages. They can be given to students to work individually or in pairs, or they can be used as a center activity. It is recommended that you go over each exercise with students before they begin. Discussion about the correct usage and completion of the graphic organizers is important to your students' understanding and success with the exercises.

Assign only one page at a time. If a student is having difficulty, use a blank graphic organizer to create a simpler one of the same type. Review the pages after the students have completed their work. Encourage discussion about the activities.

Display completed worksheets to show students' progress. The goal should be for students to be familiar and comfortable with graphic organizers, so that as they move forward, they will know how to use them, and will be able to concentrate on the information they contain, not the organizers themselves.

Graphic organizers can bring fun, excitement, and color into the classroom. Have fun, and your students will too!

Acronyms

Acronyms, or acrostics, can be used to help students remember words or the order of words by creating a new word or phrase that is easy to remember. The word or phrase usually has no connection to the words being remembered; it is simply easier to remember. An acronym can be used in any content area. When students make up their own acronyms, they will be even more likely to remember them.

Here are some commonly used acronyms:

Social Studies

The compass points:

N	Never
E	Eat
S	Sour
W	Watermelons

The Great Lakes:

H	Huron
O	Ontario
M	Michigan
E	Erie
S	Superior

Math

An order of operations:

M	My	(Multiplication)
D	Dear	(Division)
A	Aunt	(Addition)
S	Sally	(Subtraction)

or for older students:

P	Please	(Parentheses)
E	Excuse	(Exponents)
M	My	(Multiplication)
D	Dear	(Division)
A	Aunt	(Addition)
S	Sally	(Subtraction)

or:

P	Parentheses
E	Exponents
M	Multiplication
D	Division
A	Addition
S	Subtraction

Science

The order of the planets from the Sun:

Mercury	My
Venus	Very
Earth	Efficient
Mars	Mother
Jupiter	Just
Saturn	Served
Uranus	Us
Neptune	Nine
Pluto	Pizzas!

The order of the colors in a prism, or the rainbow (said like a man's name):

R	Red
O	Orange
Y	Yellow
G.	Green
B	Blue
I	Indigo
V	Violet

Music

The notes on a musical scale:

FACE, and

E	Every	or	Every
G	Good		Good
B	Boy		Boy
D	Does		Deserves
F	Fine		Fudge

Other Mnemonic Strategies

Mnemonic strategies are strategies to help students remember facts and information. It is important to note that while these strategies help students to recall facts, they may not ensure that students understand what the facts mean. However, using some of the following methods to help students remember will set a foundation on which they can build further learning.

Some things to remember when using mnemonic strategies are:

- That they be meaningful—for example, if a song is used, it should be one that the students are already familiar with, and that students at that age would know.

- That they be interesting—visuals should be colorful and draw students' attention.

- That they be repeated—bring students' attention back to the rhyme, picture, or object often, until students think of it naturally. These devices require remembering, too, but they should be easier to remember because they are fun, unique, and meaningful to the students.

The following are examples of some commonly used mnemonic strategies.

Rhyming and Songs

Some rhymes have been part of our learning for many years. Two examples are: The alphabet song, "ABCDEFG…" and "*i* before *e*, except after *c*, or when it says *a* as in *neighbor* and *weigh*." Of course, we all remember this rhyme: "Columbus sailed the ocean blue in fourteen hundred ninety-two."

A popular song to help social studies students remember the continents goes to the tune of "London Bridge": "North and South America,/Asia,/Africa, /Europe and Australia,/and Antarctica!"

Fun Stories

Funny stories can be created around a list of words to help students remember. If you have a list of vocabulary words, for example, students can write the list on a piece of paper. Then, they can build a silly story around the words. Remembering the story will be easy for them, and the words will all be there!

Chunking

Learning information in chunks, or groups of similar things, helps students remember large amounts of information. Rather than remembering all types of trees, for example, students can divide the trees into subgroups. The groups may include deciduous, evergreen, and conifer trees. Students can see how the members of each group are alike and how each group is like or different from the other groups. When learning the history of another culture, the history can be broken down into subgroups such as food, clothing, transportation, government, and customs. These smaller groups can then be put together into a meaningful picture of the way life used to be.

Visuals

Giving students a picture to recall will help them remember information and concepts. Visual imagery, hand-in-hand with the subject matter, has always had an impact on students' learning. Pictures give students something more tangible to remember and give more meaning to an unfamiliar word or concept.

Concrete Objects

Artifacts, costumes, and representations (such as props) may all be used. Students not only have a chance to see the object but can use other senses. When studying the Far East, students could smell and taste spices. They could compare foods with and without spices. Touching, smelling, and tasting objects as well as seeing them, will have an impact that hearing about things alone can never have. Representations, such as three cardboard ships for Columbus' journey, will reinforce the learning of that lesson.

Correlation to Curriculum/Student Pages

Page	Social Studies	Science & Health	Language Arts	Math	History
8			X		X
9	X		X		
11		X	X		
12		X	X		
14		X	X		
15			X		
17		X			
18		X			
20		X			
21		X	X		
23				X	
24				X	
26				X	
28				X	
29				X	
30				X	
32		X	X		
33		X	X		
35			X		
36			X		
37			X	X	
39		X	X		
40				X	
42		X	X		
43		X	X	X	
45		X	X		
46			X		
48			X		
49			X		X
51			X		
53			X		
54		X			
56		X			
57		X			
59				X	
60				X	
61				X	
63				X	
64				X	
65				X	
67				X	
68			X	X	
70		X		X	
72			X	X	
73			X	X	
75	X			X	
76		X		X	
78				X	X
79				X	X
81				X	
83	X				
84	X				X
85	X				
86	X	X			
87	X				X
89	X				
90			X		X
92			X		
93		X	X		

Dear Parent,

During this school year, our class will be integrating graphic organizers into our curriculum. These organizers—charts and tables, diagrams, time lines, maps, and memory aids—will help your child to acquire the skills necessary to do well on standard assessments. Graphic organizers are an important part of your child's learning in every subject at school. In the third grade, our goal is to improve students' skills with many different types of graphic organizers and to have students practice interpreting and creating simple graphic organizers.

From time to time, I may send activity sheets home. Please be assured that these exercises have been discussed in class, and I feel that the students are familiar enough with the exercises to work independently. To help your child do his or her best work, please consider the following suggestions:

• Provide a quiet place to work.
• Go over the worksheet together. This will help to refocus your child on the lesson and what was discussed in class.
• Encourage your child to do his or her best.
• Check the lesson when it is complete. Note improvements as well as problems.
• Let your child know that "best effort" is all that is required. If your child is having problems with the exercise after trying his or her best, we will address them in class.

Help your child maintain a positive attitude about graphic organizers. They can add interest and fun to schoolwork and should be considered a challenge, not a chore. Enjoy this time you spend with your child. With your support, graphic organizers will become useful, important tools in your child's education.

Thank you for your support.

Sincerely,

Name _____

Date _____

K	W	H	L
What do I **KNOW**?	What do I **WANT** to know?	**HOW** will I learn?	What did I **LEARN**?

K	W	H	L
What do I **KNOW**?	What do I **WANT** to know?	**HOW** will I learn?	What did I **LEARN**?
I know there is a statue near the library in my town. I know that my town is very old.	I want to know who the statue is and why it is there. I want to know how my town began. I want to know how old my town is.	I will go to the library. I will go to my town hall. I will go on my town's Internet site.	The statue is of James Smith, a soldier in the Revolutionary War. My town became a town in 1738. It was settled because some families wanted to start a new church here. They did not like the church in their old town. The first church is still here!

Near and Far

A **KWHL chart** helps you to focus on what you want to learn. First, you think of something you would like to know more about. Then, in the **K** column, you write what you already know. In the **W** column, you write what you would like to know. In the **H** column, you tell where you will look for information. In the **L** column, you write what you have learned.

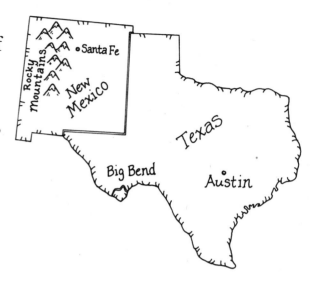

Directions Choose one of these activities. Use the blank KWHL chart on page 7 to complete the activity.

Activity 1:

What do you know about your own town or city? What would you like to know? Fill in the **K**, **W**, and **H** columns in the chart. Find out about your town. Then, fill in the **L** column.

Activity 2:

Is there another state you would like to know more about? Choose a state that you have never lived in. Then, fill in the **K**, **W**, and **H** columns in the chart. Find out about the state you chose. Then, fill in the **L** column.

Activity 3:

Do you ever wonder what life is like in other countries? What country would you like to know more about? Choose another country to learn about. Then, fill in the **K**, **W**, and **H** columns in the chart. Find out about the country. Then, fill in the **L** column.

Name _____

Date _____

K Knowledge	**Q** Questions	**L** Learning

K Knowledge	**Q** Questions	**L** Learning
People tell the weather on television and on the radio. Weather people use maps. Sometimes the weather is not what the weather people think it will be.	How do people learn to tell the weather? How do the weather people know what the weather will be? How do the maps help them?	People who tell the weather are scientists called meteorologists. They go to college to study the weather. The maps show the meteorologists what the weather is doing around the world. Radar maps that show moving weather systems show which way the weather is going and how fast. This is how meteorologists know when the weather will come to us.

Where Did They Go?

A **KQL chart** helps you to focus on what you want to learn. First, you think of something you would like to know more about. Then, in the **K** column, you write what you already know. In the **Q** column, you write what you would like to know. In the **L** column, you write what you have learned.

Directions Choose one of these activities. Use the blank KQL chart on page 10 to complete the activity.

Activity 1:

Hairy mammoths lived many years ago. Find out more about them.

Activity 2:

Dinosaurs were reptiles that lived many years ago. Find out more about one kind of dinosaur.

Activity 3:

The dodo was a bird that is now extinct. Find out what happened to the dodo.

Cool! Draw a picture of the animal you learned about. Use your chart to write a sentence telling about it.

_____

_____

_____

_____

_____

Name _____

Date _____

P Pluses (+)	M Minuses (−)	I Things I Found Interesting

P	M	I
Pluses (+)	**Minuses (–)**	**Things I Found Interesting**
I liked visiting the greenhouse because the plants were so green and healthy. I loved seeing all of the colors of the flowers.	It was kind of stuffy in the greenhouse. The plants need the air to be warm and moist, but I didn't want to stay in it too long!	I liked the way the sprayers kept the plants watered and moist. It was interesting to see how the greenhouse kept the right temperature for the plants. It didn't get too hot or too cold.

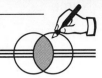

Let's Think!

A **PMI chart** organizes your thoughts. You can use a PMI chart to tell what you liked about something (Pluses), what you did not like (Minuses), and what you found interesting.

Directions Choose one of these activities. Use the blank PMI chart on page 13 to complete the activity.

Activity 1:

Tell about a movie that you saw.

Activity 2:

Tell about a book that you read or that was read to you.

Activity 3:

Tell about a trip that you have taken with your school or your family.

Cool!

Share your chart with a classmate or family member. Try to find someone who has seen the same movie, read the same book, or gone to the same place that you wrote about. Do you agree or disagree about it? Write a sentence telling what you both thought was the same or different.

Name _____ Date _____

Characteristics (What They Have or Do)		

Things to Compare

	Characteristics (What They Have or Do)		
Things to Compare	**Place to Play**	**Equipment**	**Number of Players**
Basketball	Court (indoors or outdoors)	Basket(s) 1 Ball	1 to 5 on each team
Tennis	Court (indoors or outdoors)	Net Racket 2 or 3 Balls	1 or 2 on each team
Soccer	Field (indoors or outdoors)	1 Soccer ball Nets	11 on each team
Football	Field (outdoors)	1 Football Goals	11 on each team

Name _____ Date _____

Amazing Animals

Animals have different ways to stay alive and safe in winter. You can see how animals are alike or different by using a chart.

Directions Look at this chart. See what bears, whales, snowshoe rabbits, geese, and monarch butterflies do in the winter. Then, answer the questions.

		Characteristics (What They Have or Do)		
		Move (Migrate)	Sleep (Hibernate)	Change Color (Camouflage)
Things to Compare	Bear	no	yes	no
	Whale	yes	no	no
	Snowshoe Rabbit	no	no	yes
	Canadian Goose	yes	no	no
	Monarch Butterfly	yes	no	no

1. What does a whale do in the winter?

_____

2. How does a snowshoe rabbit protect itself in the winter?

_____

3. Which animal hibernates in the winter?

_____

4. What three animals move to a warmer place in the winter?

_____

_____

5. Choose five other animals. Use the blank chart on page 16 to compare and contrast three characteristics. You may use the same characteristics that are on the chart above, cr you may choose your own.

Name _____

Date _____

Things to Compare
How Are They Alike/Different?

Things to Compare				
Trait 1:				
Trait 2:				
Trait 3:				
Trait 4:				

Things to Compare
How Are They Alike/Different?

	Shark	Whale
Trait 1: Type of animal	A shark is a fish.	A whale is a mammal.
Trait 2: Way of having babies	Shark babies (pups) hatch from eggs while still inside the mother. Then, they come out as little sharks.	Whale babies (calves) are born live. They do not hatch from eggs.
Trait 3: Breathing	Sharks get air from the water through their gills.	Whales need to surface to get air into their lungs.
Trait 4: Habitat	Sharks live in the ocean.	Whales live in the ocean.

Charts & Tables: Compare & Contrast Matrix
Graphic Organizers Across the Curriculum 3, SV 3416-9

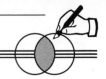

Alike or Different?

A **comparison and contrast chart** helps you to see how things are alike or different.

For example, you may have a sister or a brother. How are you two alike? Are your eyes the same color? Do you both have brown hair? Do you both like to play games? These are all **traits** that tell about you and your sister or brother.

Directions ▶ Choose one of these activities. Decide what your two items will be. Write them in the blanks. Then, think of four traits to compare between the two items. Write the traits in the blanks. Think about how the items are alike and how they are different. Complete the blank comparison chart on page 19 using the items and traits you chose.

1. Compare two plants. It may help you to find pictures of the plants.

Plant 1: _____

Plant 2: _____

Trait 1: _____

Trait 2: _____

Trait 3: _____

Trait 4: _____

2. Compare a room in your home with a room in your school.

Room 1: _____

Room 2: _____

Trait 1: _____

Trait 2: _____

Trait 3: _____

Trait 4: _____

Date _____

Name _____

Favorite Winter Activity

Name	Sliding	Skating	Skiing
Renee	X	yes	X
James	yes	X	X
Cami	X	X	yes

Favorite Foods

Name	Pizza	Tacos	Chicken Fingers	Spaghetti
Carlos	X	X	yes	X
Ashley	X	yes	X	X
Jeff	yes	X	X	X
Jessica	X	X	X	yes

Charts & Tables: Logic Table
Graphic Organizers Across the Curriculum 3, SV 3416-9

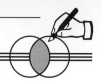

That Makes Sense

A **logic table** can help you find an answer when you don't have all the facts.

Look at the example table. What is each student's favorite activity?

Sue likes to do crafts. There is a **Yes** under Crafts for Sue. Put an **X** under Puzzles and Models for Sue.

Tom likes to do Puzzles. There is a **Yes** under Puzzles for Tom. Put an **X** under Models and Crafts for Tom.

You can put an **X** under Puzzles and Crafts for Zoe. This means that Zoe likes to make models. Put a **Yes** under Models for Zoe.

	Puzzles	Models	Crafts
Sue			yes
Tom	yes		
Zoe			

Directions ▶ Use the blank logic table on the bottom of page 22. Label the chart across the top: **Library**, **Museum**, **Park**, and **Aquarium**. Write **Greg**, **Lisa**, **Ben**, and **Sara** in the left-hand column. This is what you know: Greg likes to look at art. Ben likes to run and play. Sara is interested in sharks.

Name _____ Date _____

	1	2	3	4	5	6	7	8	9	10
1										
2										
3										
4										
5										
6										
7										
8										
9										
10										

www.svschoolsupply.com
© Steck-Vaughn Company

Charts & Tables: Addition Grid
Graphic Organizers Across the Curriculum 3, SV 3416-9

Chart for a Start!

Directions This chart can be used for addition or subtraction. Fill in the missing numbers. Then, use the finished chart to complete the problems.

	1	2	3	4	5	6	7	8	9	10
1	2	3	4	5	6	7	8	9	10	11
2	3	4	5	6	7	8	9	10	11	12
3										
4										
5										
6										
7										
8										
9										
10										

1. $4 + 8 =$ _____

2. $7 + 3 =$ _____

3. $4 + 10 =$ _____

4. $12 - 2 =$ _____

5. $9 - 3 =$ _____

6. $15 - 7 =$ _____

Name _____   Date _____

Day				

Time					

Bakery Specials

Day of Special					
Time It Will Be Ready	**Monday**	**Tuesday**	**Wednesday**	**Thursday**	**Friday**
8:00	Muffins	Bagels	Donuts	Cinnamon Buns	Donuts
10:00	Quick Breads		Cookies		
11:00		Pies		Quick Breads	Cakes
12:00	Cakes		Cupcakes	Pies	
2:00	Dinner Rolls	French Bread	Italian Bread	Biscuits	Pizza Bread

School Schedule

Class	Time Begins	Time Ends
Spelling	10:00	10:30
Reading	10:30	11:00
Math	11:00	11:30
Science	1:00	2:00

www.svschoolsupply.com
© Steck-Vaughn Company

Charts & Tables: Schedules
Graphic Organizers Across the Curriculum 3, SV 3416-9

TV Time

A **schedule** is a list of times for doing things. Look at this schedule. It lists programs that will be on television between 4:00 P.M. and 8:00 P.M.

Channel	4:00	4:30	5:00	5:30	6:00	6:30	7:00	7:30
2	Pay the Price	Strike Out	Police Boat		Spectacular Hour of Superheroes		O'Hara & Garcia	News
5	The Red Stallion	Lori Lee, M.D.	The Wilsons	Cooking with Emma	News		TV Classics	
8	Melvin's Island	Movie: *Queen Kong*			News		Hollywood Now	Head to Head
10	Student Life		Wheel of Money	Dial a Date	News		Adventure Tales	

Directions ➤ Use the schedule to answer each question.

1. When can you watch *Wheel of Money*?

_____

2. When can you watch *Student Life*?

_____

3. On which channel is there no news program at 6:00?

_____

4. How many hours is the movie *Queen Kong*?

_____

5. Which channel has the most programs between 4:00 and 7:00?

_____

6. Which channel has the fewest programs between 4:00 and 7:00?

_____

7. What show is on Channel 5 one hour before the News?

_____

8. What show starts on Channel 2 three and a half hours before the News?

_____

Scheduling Time

Carrie made a plan for how she would spend her time after school.

Carrie started to make a schedule for her activities. She gets home from school at 3:00.

Each activity begins when the activity before it ends.

Activity	Elapsed Time
Snack	15 minutes
Walk dog	15 minutes
Homework	45 minutes
Play outside	1 hour
Read	30 minutes
Chores	15 minutes

Directions Use the information from Carrie's plan to complete her schedule. The first two activities are completed for you.

Activity	Start Time	End Time	Elapsed Time
Snack	**3:00**	**3:15**	**15 minutes**
Walk dog	**3:15**	**3:30**	**15 minutes**

Directions Make up a schedule that shows three activities you plan to do after school. Use the blank schedule on page 27. List the **Activity, Start Time, End Time,** and **Elapsed Time**.

Date

Name

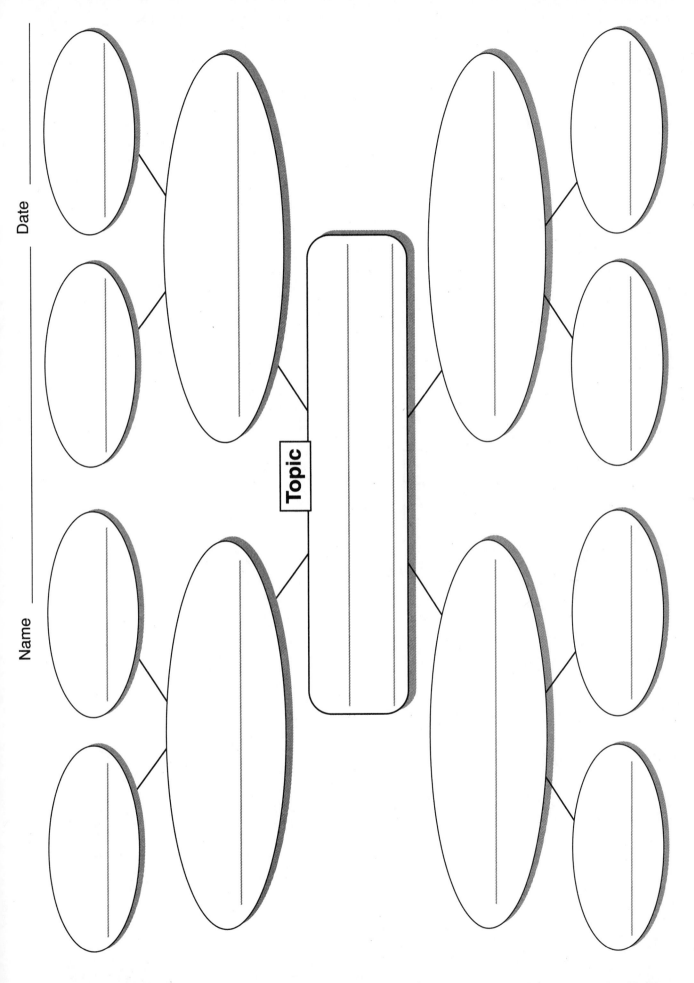

Topic

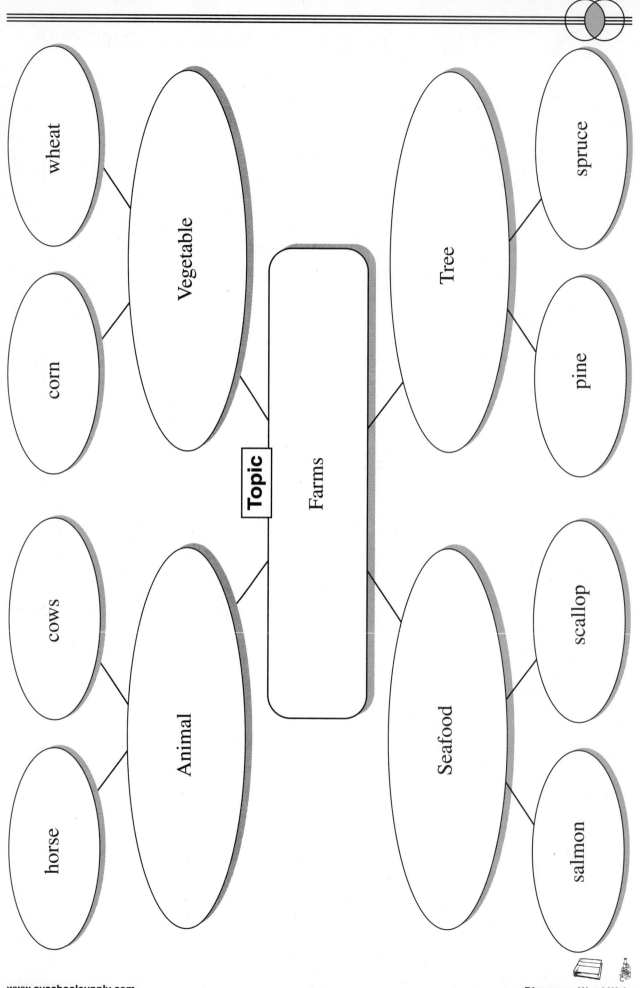

Topic

Farms

Vegetable — wheat, corn

Tree — spruce, pine

Animal — cows, horse

Seafood — scallop, salmon

www.svschoolsupply.com
© Steck-Vaughn Company

Diagrams: Word Web
Graphic Organizers Across the Curriculum 3, SV 3416-9

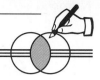

Bird's the Word

Directions Read this passage about different types of birds. Then, use the passage to complete the blank word web on page 31.

What is a bird? All birds have some things in common. They all have wings and backbones. They all have bills rather than teeth. They all breathe air and hatch from eggs with shells. Birds are warm-blooded animals.

There are many differences among birds, however. Some birds fly to warmer places for the winter. Snow geese may fly as far south as Mexico. Then, in the spring, they fly back to Canada, Alaska, and Siberia. There, they mate and hatch their young. Another migrating bird is the swan.

The ostrich has wings, but it cannot fly. In this way, ostriches are like penguins. Penguins do not fly either, but they do swim gracefully through the ocean!

Some birds are called birds of prey. They hunt and eat small animals. They have strong bills and claws to grab and tear apart their meals. Owls and eagles are birds of prey.

Many birds are water birds. They have special feathers that keep them warm in cold waters. They are good swimmers and divers, and they get their food from the water. Ducks and swans spend a lot of time in the water.

These are only a few of the many, many different types of birds in the world. There are so many interesting things to know about each and every one!

Name _____ Date _____

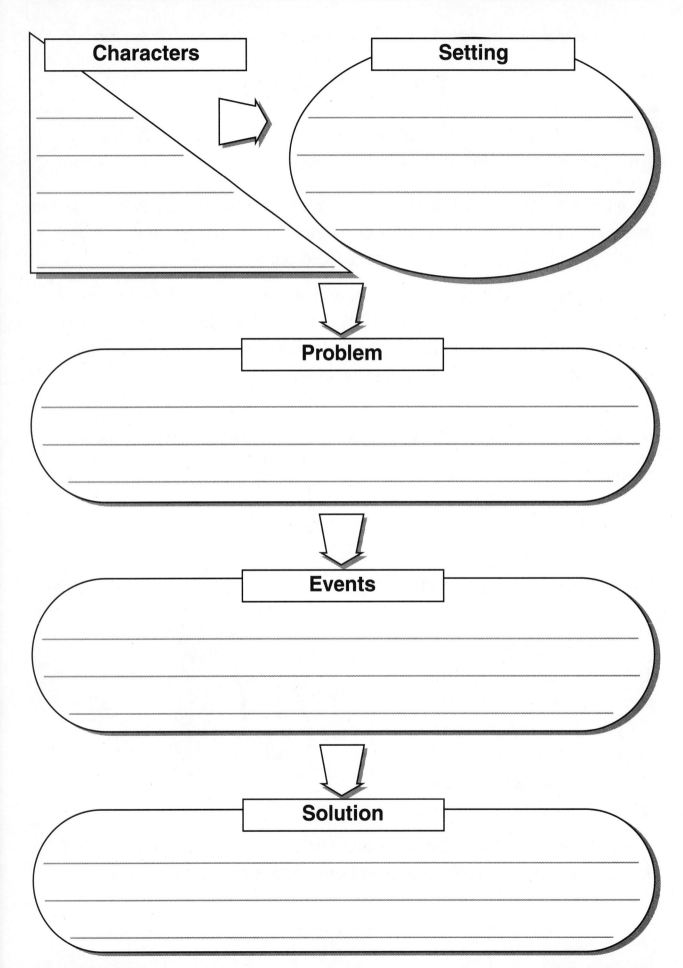

Characters

Setting

Problem

Events

Solution

www.svschoolsupply.com
© Steck-Vaughn Company

Diagrams: Story Map
Graphic Organizers Across the Curriculum 3, SV 3416-9

Characters

Little Red
Riding Hood
Grandma
Wolf

Setting

forest
Grandma's house

Problem

The wolf ate Grandma and is going to eat
Little Red Riding Hood, too.

Events

Little Red Riding Hood is bringing food to her Grandma.
She meets the wolf. The wolf goes to Grandma's and
pretends to be Grandma.

Solution

A hunter passing by sees what is happening through Grandma's
window. He kills the wolf and frees Grandma
from the wolf's stomach.

Diagrams: Story Map
Graphic Organizers Across the Curriculum 3, SV 3416-9

Emergency!

Directions Read the story. Then, use the story to complete the blank story map on page 34.

Kenny looked forward to Thanksgiving Day every year. His grandfather always came to visit. Grandpa would share stories with Kenny, and they would laugh and talk for hours.

One year after the family had eaten their Thanksgiving meal, Kenny's parents and his brother went to see a movie. Kenny and his grandfather thought about what they could do during the afternoon.

"I know," Kenny said. "Let's play football! I need a lot of practice."

"That sounds like fun," answered Grandpa. "Find the football, and I'll meet you in the yard."

Kenny and Grandpa passed the football back and forth many times. They practiced passing and catching. Suddenly, as Grandpa reached to catch a pass, he fell down.

"Grandpa, what's wrong?" asked Kenny.

"I stepped in a hole and tripped, Kenny," Grandpa answered slowly. "I think I broke my ankle. You will need to call for help."

Kenny hurried into the house to make the call. Beside the telephone he saw a list of telephone numbers. He carefully dialed the number next to the word *emergency*. A man's voice answered at the other end. He asked Kenny several questions, and Kenny answered each one.

An ambulance and Kenny's parents arrived at almost the same time. Kenny could see that Grandpa was in good hands.

"We are glad that you were here to help Grandpa," Kenny's parents said. "We are proud of you for taking such good care of him."

A Poem Can Tell a Story

Directions Read this poem. Think about the story it tells. Then, complete the blank story map on page 34.

Number Slumber *by Thomasin Heyworth*

Last night I dreamed
Things were never just one,
But numbers of things,
For a while, it was fun!

There were oodles of poodles
And vats of cats,
Groups of sloops—
And much more than that!

I saw several snakes
Slither out through a door,
And when I went, too,
I found dozens more!

There were messes of dresses
And gobs of knobs.
There were fleets of treats.
There was paint by globs!

I saw hundreds of hippos
And trucks of ducks,
Zillions of zebras
And billions of bucks!

A gazillion gorillas
Had tons of toys,
Enough for a million
Girls and boys!

Enter the elephants,
And there were so many,
That I'd have been rich
If for each I'd a penny!

But a message came
To my brain as I slept.
The words, "You must count these,"
Into my ear crept.

So I tried and I tried
To count them and yet,
I began to get anxious,
Break into a sweat!

Knee deep in sheep,
I tried to keep track
Of bunches of birds,
And yak upon yak!

I woke with a start,
A relief, I must say!
'Til I remembered the math test
That I have today.

Name _____

Date _____

A=

B=

C=

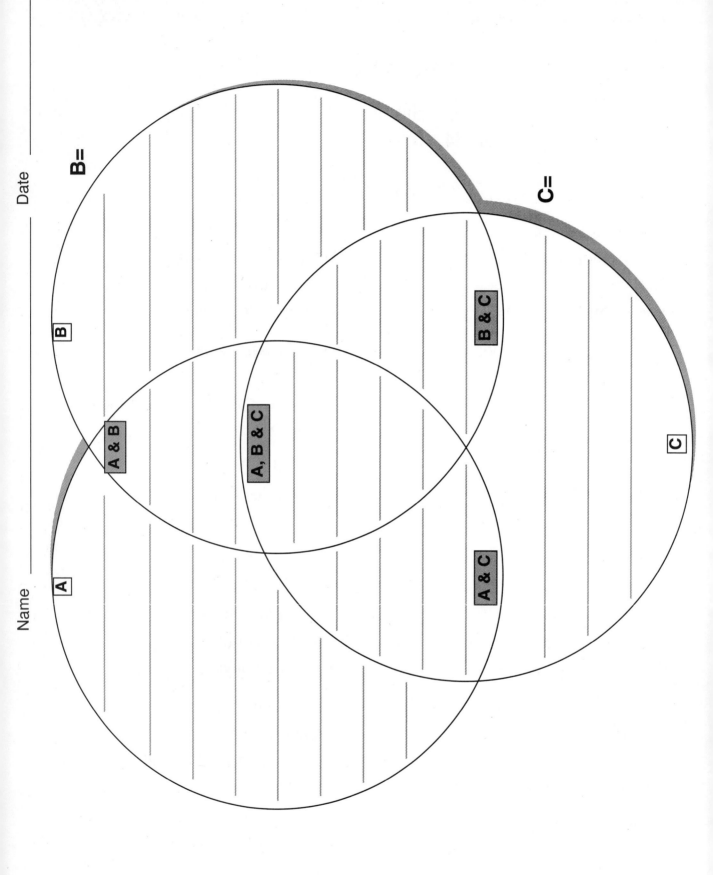

A

B

C

A & B

B & C

A & C

A, B & C

www.svschoolsupply.com
© Steck-Vaughn Company

Diagrams: Venn Diagram
Graphic Organizers Across the Curriculum 3, SV 3416-9

A= green

B= plant

C= food for people

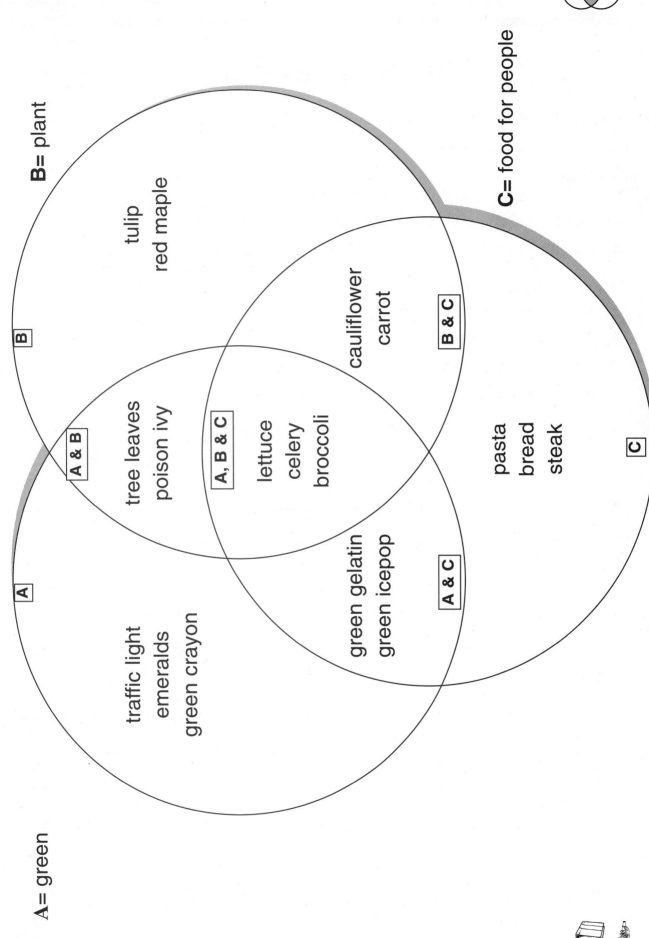

A
traffic light
emeralds
green crayon

B
tulip
red maple

A & B
tree leaves
poison ivy

A, B & C
lettuce
celery
broccoli

B & C
cauliflower
carrot

A & C
green gelatin
green icepop

C
pasta
bread
steak

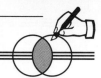

Where Does It Go?

A **Venn diagram** helps you to group things by seeing how they are alike or different.

Directions Use the blank Venn diagram on page 38. Follow the directions in 1–4. Then, use what you know to put each thing in the correct place on the diagram.

1. Write **in sky** next to **A =**.
2. Write **gives heat** next to **B =**.
3. Write **gives light** next to **C =**.
4. Think: Is it in the sky? Does it give off heat? Does it give off light? Write **yes** or **no**.

	in the sky?	gives off heat?	gives off light?
rain	_____	_____	_____
stove	_____	_____	_____
computer screen	_____	_____	_____
star	_____	_____	_____
fire	_____	_____	_____
radiator	_____	_____	_____
your body	_____	_____	_____
cloud	_____	_____	_____
light bulb	_____	_____	_____
Sun	_____	_____	_____
flashlight	_____	_____	_____
lightning	_____	_____	_____

Is there a part of the diagram that has no words in it? _____

What is it? _____

Name _____   Date _____

Word	Group	Description	Example(s)

Word	Group	Description	Example(s)
vegetable	plant	grows in gardens, often crunchy, good to eat	carrots, beans, turnips, potatoes
cactus	plant	grows in desert, many sizes, needs little water	prickly pear, saguaro
flower	plant	can be wild or grow in garden, beautiful blooms	roses, daisies, mums, violets, marigolds, tulips
tree	plant	large plants, have leaves or needles, homes for animals	pine, oak, maple, poplar, magnolia

Diagrams: Vocabulary Grid
Graphic Organizers Across the Curriculum 3, SV 3416-9

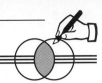

Something in Common

Directions Use the words in one of these exercises to complete the blank chart on page 41. Then, make a sentence for each word you chose.

1. addition _____

_____

subtraction _____

_____

multiplication _____

_____

division _____

_____

2. mammal _____

_____

reptile _____

_____

fish _____

_____

bird _____

_____

Diagrams: Completing a Vocabulary Grid
Graphic Organizers Across the Curriculum 3, SV 3416-9

Name _____ Date _____

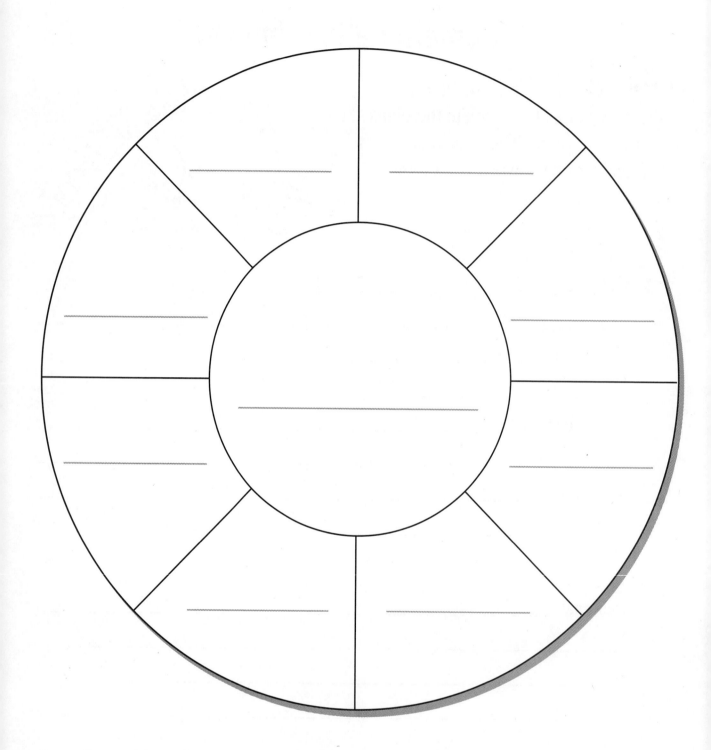

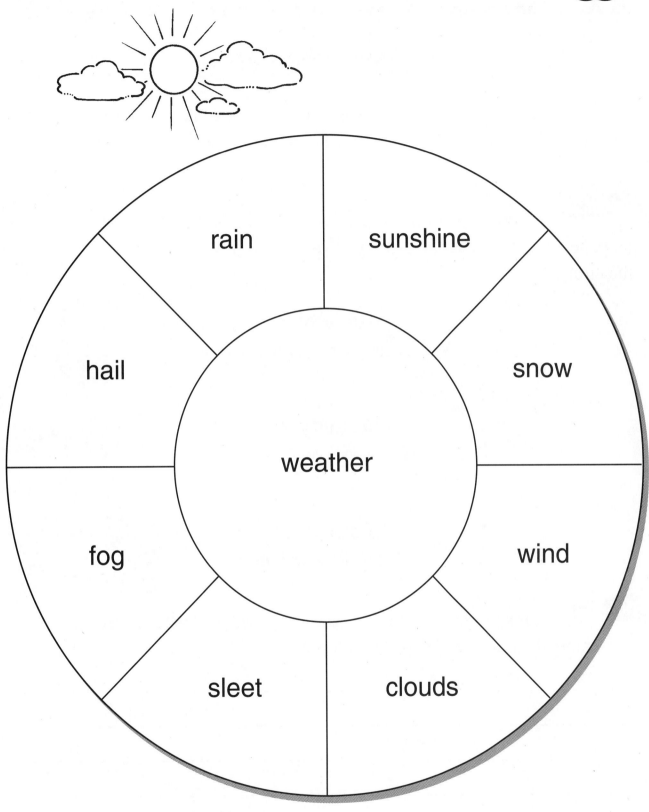

rain

sunshine

hail

snow

weather

fog

wind

sleet

clouds

Diagrams: Word Wheel
Graphic Organizers Across the Curriculum 3, SV 3416-9

Free Wheeler

A **word wheel** helps you to expand your thinking. The center of the wheel shows your main idea. Coming out from the center, you list thoughts that come from the main idea.

Directions Choose one of these activities. Use the blank word wheel on page 44 to complete the activity. Write the bold word in the center of the circle.

Activity 1:
Write about your favorite **activities**.

Activity 2:
Write about your **school**.

Activity 3:
Write about your **family**.

Directions Choose one of the words you wrote on your wheel. Write a paragraph about it. Use complete sentences.

_____

_____

_____

_____

_____

_____

_____

Name _____   Date _____

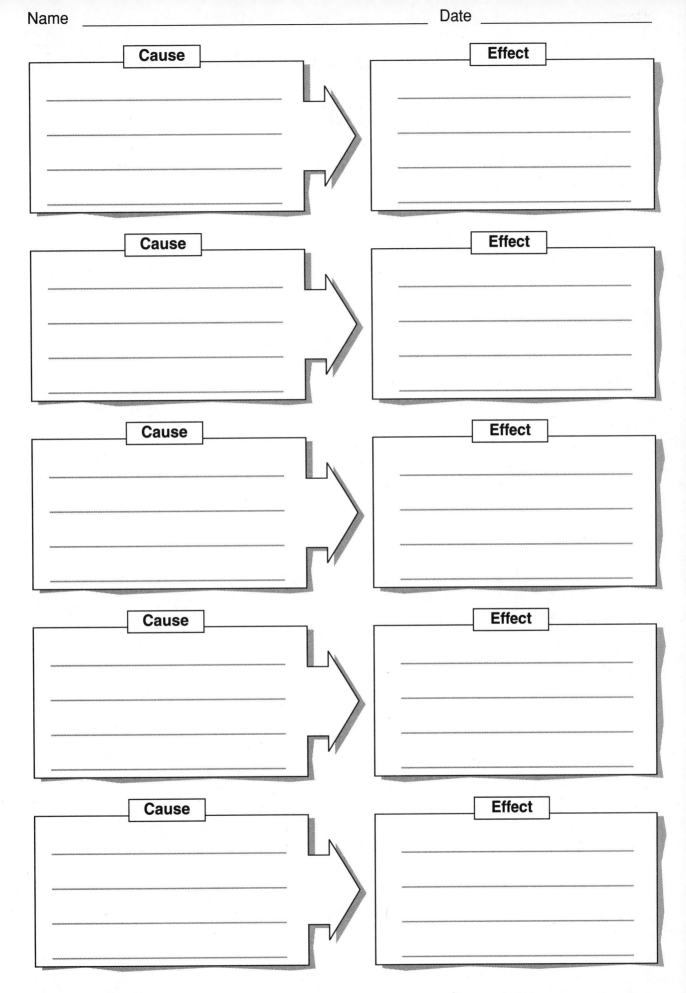

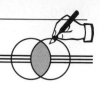

Find Out Why

A **cause** is what makes something happen, or why it happens. An **effect** is what happens. Read the following sentence. See if you can tell which is the cause and which is the effect.

The step was icy, so Jenny slipped.

What is the cause? The cause is that the step was icy. What is the effect? The effect is that Jenny slipped.

Directions Read these sentences. Write the cause and effect in the correct boxes on page 47.

1. Because the weather was bad, school was cancelled.

2. Scott and Joey stopped to play on the way to the bus stop, so the bus left without them.

3. There was a big party for Julie because it was her birthday.

4. Juan waited a long time to get a new puppy, so he was very happy when his mother brought one home.

5. Nina did not eat breakfast, so she felt hungry.

Cause

Someone left the door open.

Effect

The puppy got out of the house.

Cause

The ice cream sat in the Sun.

Effect

The ice cream melted.

Effect 1

People could stay warm.

Cause

People found out how to make fire.

Effect 2

People could cook their food.

Effect 3

People could send smoke signals.

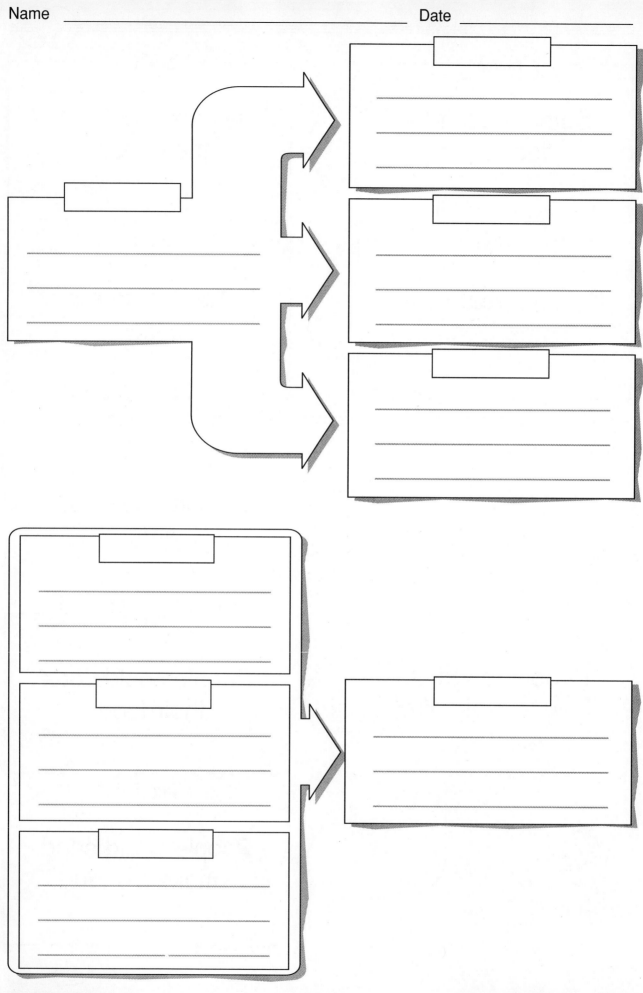

More than One

A **cause** is what makes something happen, or why it happens. An **effect** is what happens. Sometimes there is more than one cause or more than one effect. This paragraph shows one cause and three effects.

The car was not working. Becky couldn't get to her friend's house. Joe couldn't get to work. Danielle couldn't get to her class.

Directions ▶ Read these paragraphs. Decide if there is more than one cause or more than one effect. Use the blank cause and effect diagrams on page 50. Label the single box **cause** or **effect**. Label the three boxes as causes or effects. Write the sentences in the correct boxes.

1. If you eat a healthy diet, you will feel better. You will also look better, and you will have more energy.

2. The electricity was out. The telephone wire was broken. There was water over the road. Jeremy could not get in touch with his family.

Date _____

Name _____

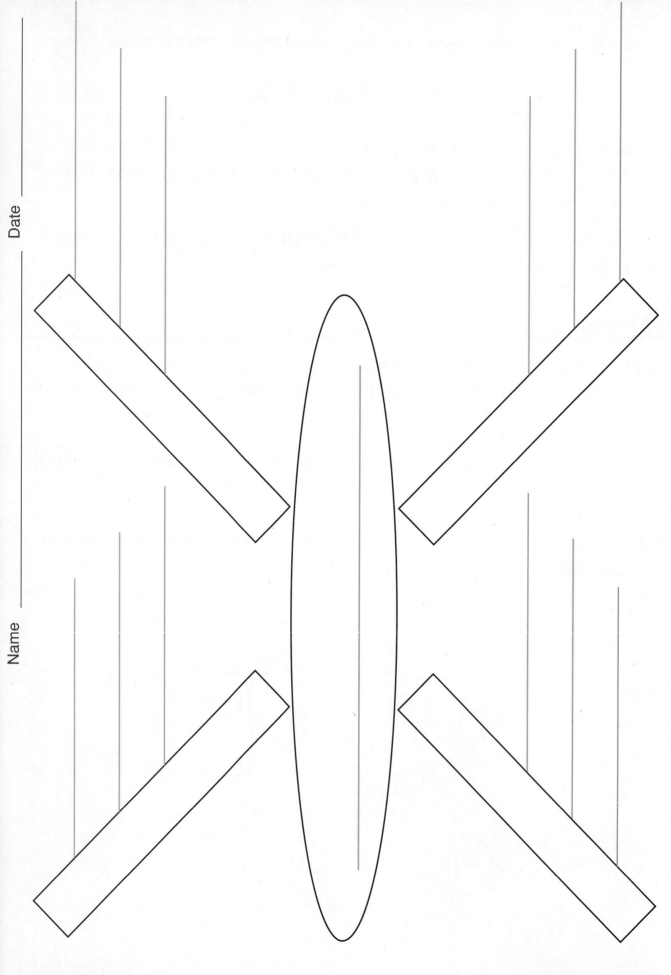

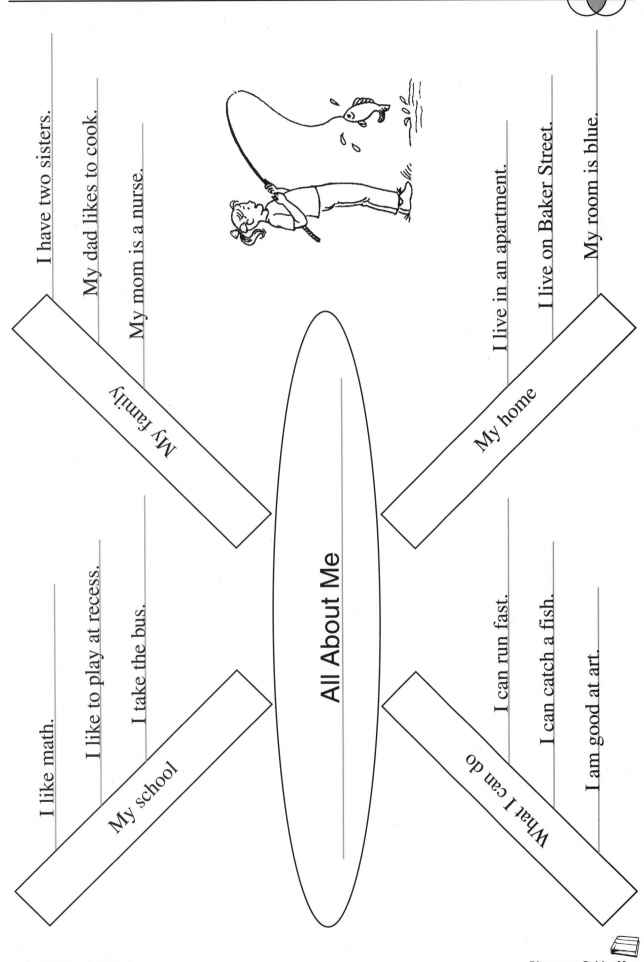

All About Me

My family
- I have two sisters.
- My dad likes to cook.
- My mom is a nurse.

My home
- I live in an apartment.
- I live on Baker Street.
- My room is blue.

My school
- I like math.
- I like to play at recess.
- I take the bus.

What I can do
- I can run fast.
- I can catch a fish.
- I am good at art.

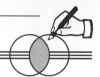

Favorites

A **spider map** can help you to organize your ideas.
The spider's "body" is your subject. The spider's "legs"
are each a part of the subject.

Directions ▶ Choose one of these activities. Use the blank
spider map on page 52 to complete the activity.

Activity 1:

What are your favorite healthy foods? On the spider's "body," write
healthy foods. On each "leg" of the spider, write one of these groups:

Fruits and Vegetables

Grains and Cereals

Dairy

Meats/Proteins

Then, on each line coming off each leg, write your favorite foods from
that group. For example, on the leg that says "Dairy," you might write
"yogurt." You may want to use a Food Pyramid to help you.

Activity 2:

What are your favorite activities? On the spider's "body," write **activities**.
On each "leg" of the spider, write one of your favorite activities.

Then, on each line coming off each leg, write what you like
about the activity. For example, if a leg says "Baseball," you
might write "batting" and "running the bases."

Name _____   Date _____

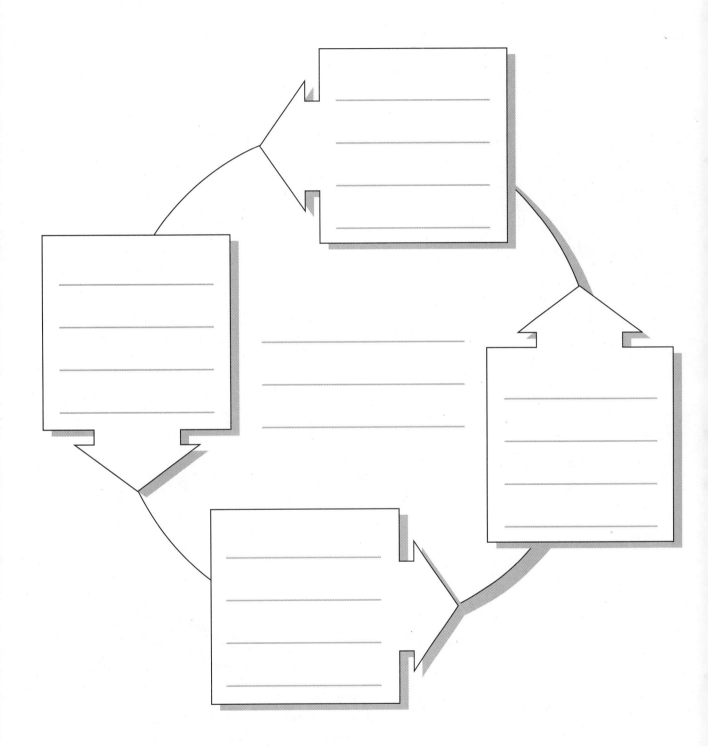

A frog begins as an egg.

Then, the frog grows a tail. It is a tadpole.

Life Cycle of a Frog

Now the frog can go on land or in water. It can lay eggs.

Then, it grows legs and loses its tail.

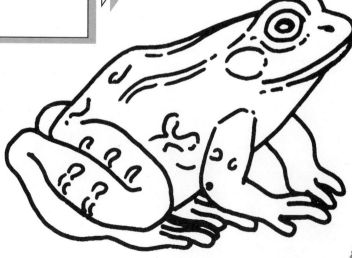

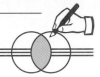

Track the Changes

A **cycle diagram** shows how things change over time. Many things have cycles. A washing machine has cycles. So does nature!

Directions Choose one of the activities below. Use the blank cycle diagram on page 55 to complete the activity you chose.

Activity 1:

Did you know that a butterfly was once a caterpillar? All butterflies begin as caterpillars. Then, they go through changes to become butterflies. Each change has a special name.

Look in a book or on the Internet. Find out about butterflies and how they grow. Then, fill in the boxes in the cycle diagram to tell the name of each different part of a butterfly's life. Be sure to put the parts in order. Then, draw a picture near each box to show how that part looks.

Activity 2:

The moon seems to have many shapes. The changing shapes are called the phases of the moon. Find out about the phases of the moon. There are four main phases. Write the name of each phase on the cycle diagram. Be sure to put the phases in order. Then, draw a picture near each box to show how the moon looks in the sky during each phase.

Name _____

Date _____

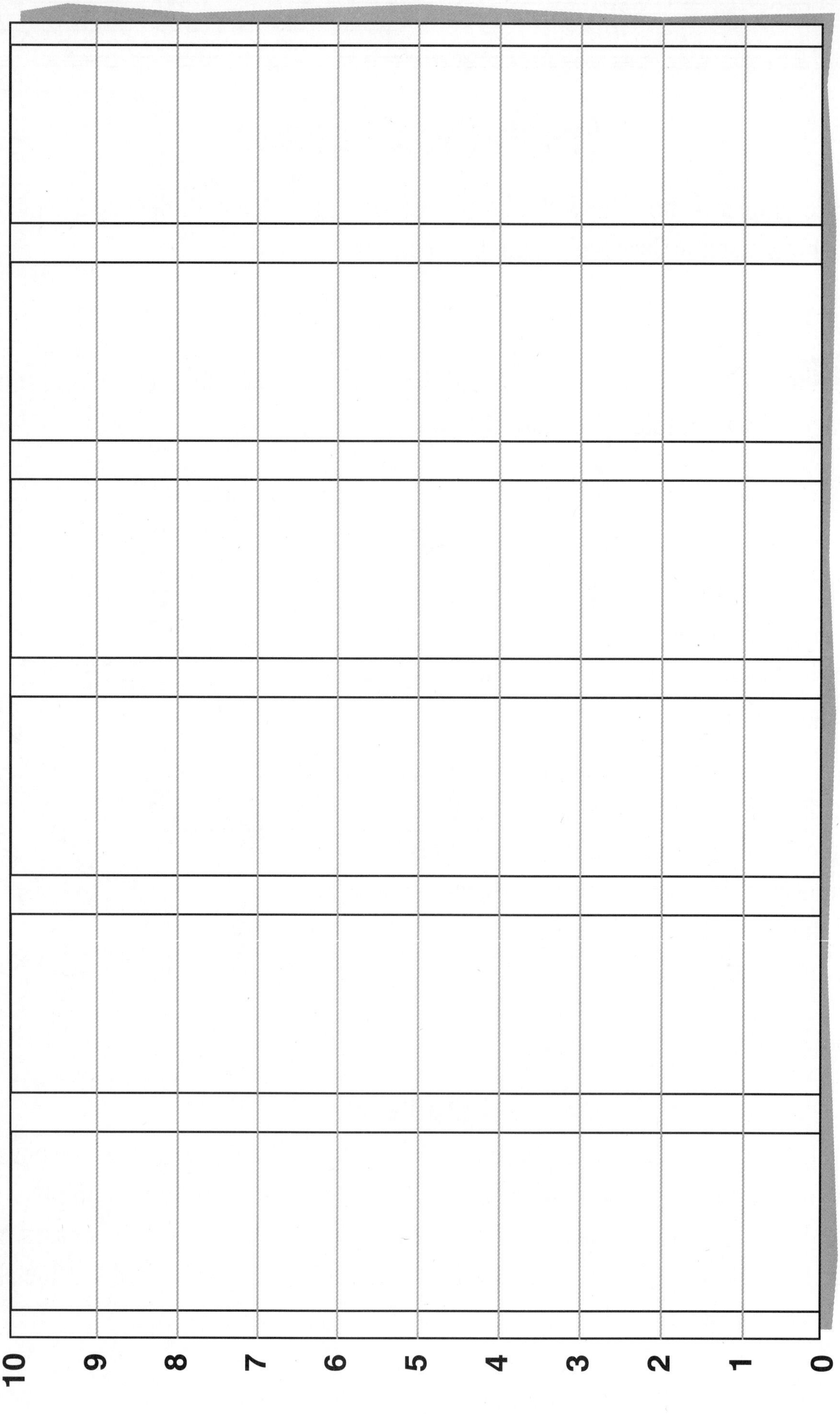

10
9
8
7
6
5
4
3
2
1
0

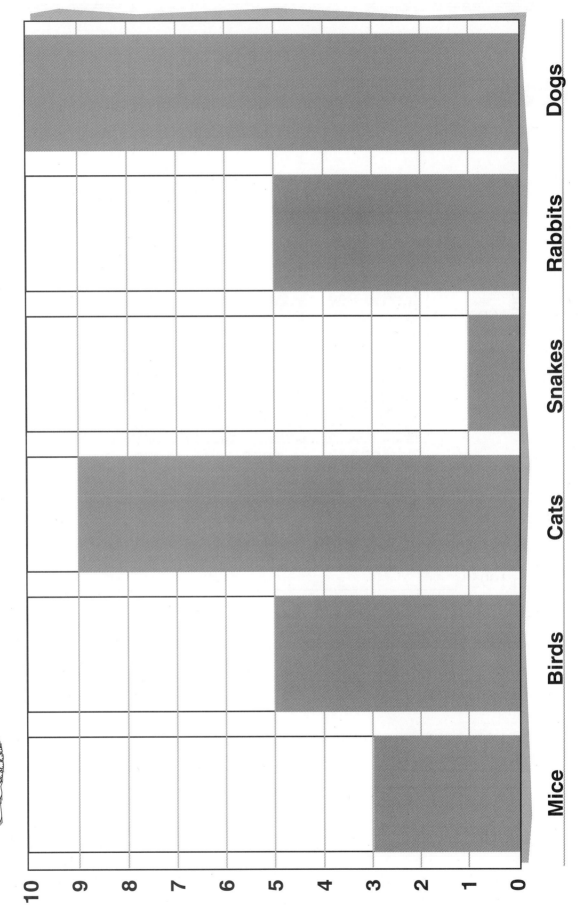

Number of Students with Each Pet

	Dogs	Rabbits	Snakes	Cats	Birds	Mice
10						
9	■			■		
8	■			■		
7	■			■		
6	■			■		
5	■	■		■	■	
4	■	■		■	■	
3	■	■		■	■	■
2	■	■		■	■	■
1	■	■	■	■	■	■
0						

Graphs: Vertical Bar Graph
Graphic Organizers Across the Curriculum 3, SV 3416-9

Tax Facts

Directions → Look at the bar graph. It shows how much tax money Biggsville spent on its schools. Use the graph to answer the questions.

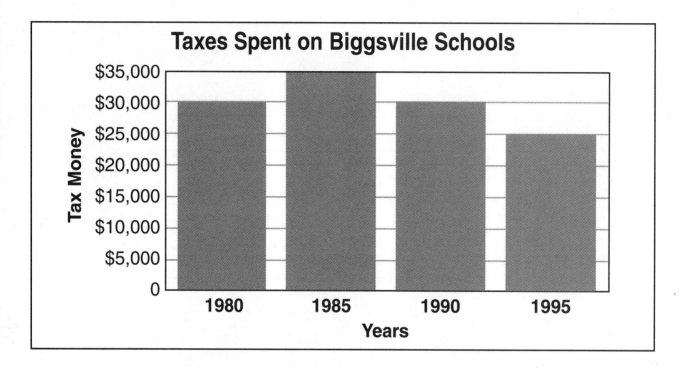

1. How much tax money did Biggsville spend on schools in 1980? _____

   In 1995? _____

2. In what year did Biggsville spend the most money? _____

   How much? _____

3. Did Biggsville spend more tax money on schools in 1980 or 1995?

   _____

4. How much more money did Biggsville spend on schools in 1990 than in 1995?

   _____

Graph It

Directions Choose one of these activities to do with a partner. After you have collected the information, use the blank vertical bar graph on page 58 to make your own graph. Be sure to give your graph a title.

Activity 1:

What are your classmates' favorite games? Take a survey, and write down all of the answers. Add up the totals for each game. Choose the five most popular games to put on your graph. Put the rest of the games under "Other" with their total number.

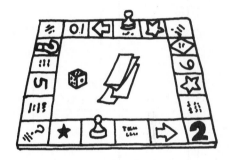

Activity 2:

What are your classmates' favorite pets? Take a survey, and write down all of the answers. Add up the totals for each pet. Choose the five most popular pets to put on your graph. Put the rest of the pets under "Other" with their total number.

Activity 3:

What are your classmates' favorite subjects in school? Take a survey, and write down all of the answers. Add up the totals for each subject. Choose the five most popular subjects to put on your graph. Put the rest of the subjects under "Other" with their total number.

Name

Date

0 1 2 3 4 5 6 7 8 9 10

62

Number of Student Birthdays Each Month

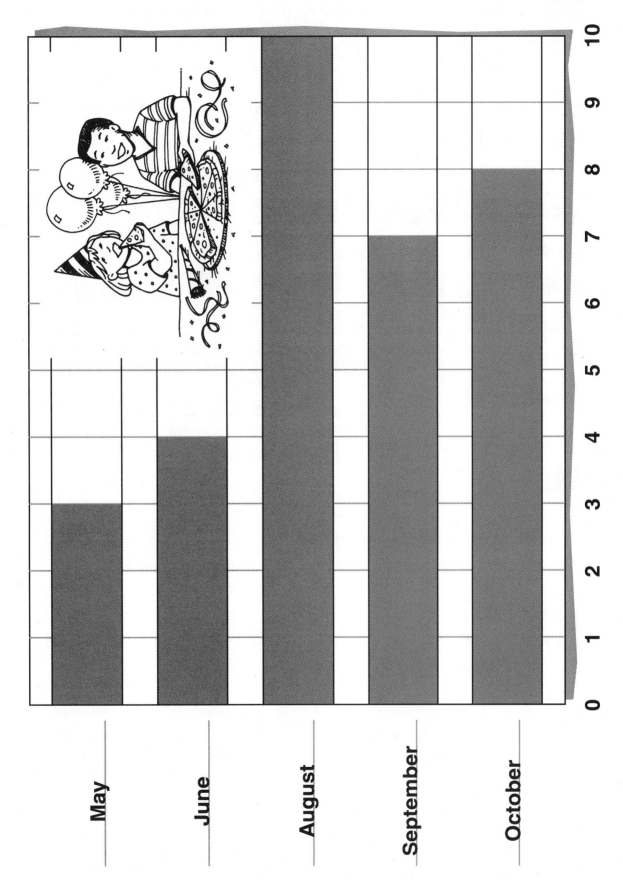

Month	Number
May	3
June	4
August	10
September	7
October	8

Graphs: Horizontal Bar Graph
Graphic Organizers Across the Curriculum 3, SV 3416-9

Ticket Costs

You can show and compare information in a **horizontal bar graph**.
The bar beside baseball ends at the $3 mark, so a baseball ticket costs $3.

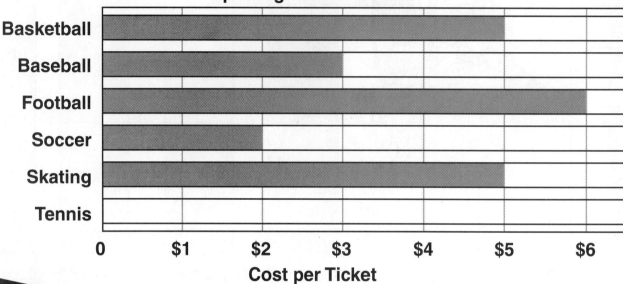

Sporting Events Tickets

Cost per Ticket

Directions Use the bar graph above to solve.

1. How much does a soccer ticket cost?

_____

2. How much does a basketball ticket cost?

_____

3. The tickets for which sporting event cost most?

_____

4. The tickets for which sporting event cost least?

_____

5. For which two sports are tickets the same price?

_____

6. How much more does a basketball ticket cost than a soccer ticket?

_____

7. Add a bar for tennis that shows a cost per ticket of $4.

8. How much less does a tennis ticket cost than a skating ticket?

_____

Graph It 2

Directions Choose one of these activities to do with a partner. After you have collected the information, use the blank horizontal bar graph on page 62 to make your own graph. Be sure to give your graph a title.

Activity 1:

What are your classmates' favorite places to visit? Take a survey, and write down all of the answers. Add up the totals for each place. Choose the five most popular places to put on your graph. Put the rest of the places under "Other" with their total number.

Activity 2:

What are your classmates' favorite foods? Take a survey, and write down all of the answers. Add up the totals for each food. Choose the five most popular foods to put on your graph. Put the rest of the foods under "Other" with their total number.

Activity 3:

What are your classmates' favorite movies? Take a survey, and write down all of the answers. Add up the totals for each movie. Choose the five most popular movies to put on your graph. Put the rest of the movies under "Other" with their total number.

Homework Turned in on Time

Jen	☆ ☆ ☆ ☆ ☆ ☆
Robert	☆ ☆
Ben	☆ ☆ ☆ ☆ ☆ ☆ ☆ ☆
Daniel	☆ ☆ ☆ ☆
Rosa	☆ ☆ ☆ ☆ ☆
Wendi	☆ ☆ ☆
Cara	☆ ☆
Alison	☆ ☆ ☆ ☆
Trish	☆ ☆
Mark	☆ ☆ ☆ ☆ ☆
David	☆ ☆

Graphs: Pictograph
Graphic Organizers Across the Curriculum 3, SV 3416-9

There's a Bear!

A **pictograph** uses pictures to show data. Each picture stands for a certain number of people or things. Sometimes the pictures stand for several or many things.

This pictograph shows the number of bears seen in a park.

Bear Sightings

Thursday	🐻	🐻	🐻	🐻	🐻				
Friday	🐻								
Saturday	🐻	🐻	🐻	🐻	🐻	🐻			
Sunday	🐻	🐻	🐻	🐻	🐻	🐻	🐻	🐻	
Monday	🐻	🐻	🐻	🐻					

Each 🐻 = 2 bears

Directions ➤ Use the graph to answer these questions.

1. What is the title of the pictograph? _____

2. How many bears does each picture stand for? _____

3. How many bears were seen on Saturday? _____

4. Were more bears seen on Thursday or Monday? _____

5. Use the blank pictograph on page 66 to make your own graph. Give it a title. Write three questions about your graph. Trade questions and graphs with a classmate.

69

Connect the Dots

This is a **line graph**. It shows how many living things some students found at a pond. On Monday, the students found one living thing. How many did they find on Wednesday?

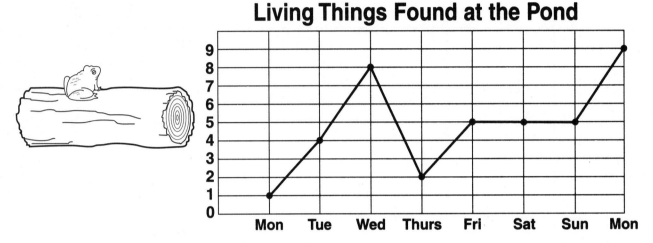

Living Things Found at the Pond

Once a month, students at Cray School collect trash around their town. They keep track of the number of pounds of trash they collect.

September	65 pounds
October	40 pounds
November	20 pounds
December	25 pounds
January	15 pounds
February	12 pounds
March	20 pounds
April	35 pounds
May	40 pounds

Directions Use what you know to make a line graph. Use the blank graph on page 69. Give the graph a title. Then, write three questions about the graph. Trade questions and graphs with a classmate.

Name _____   Date _____

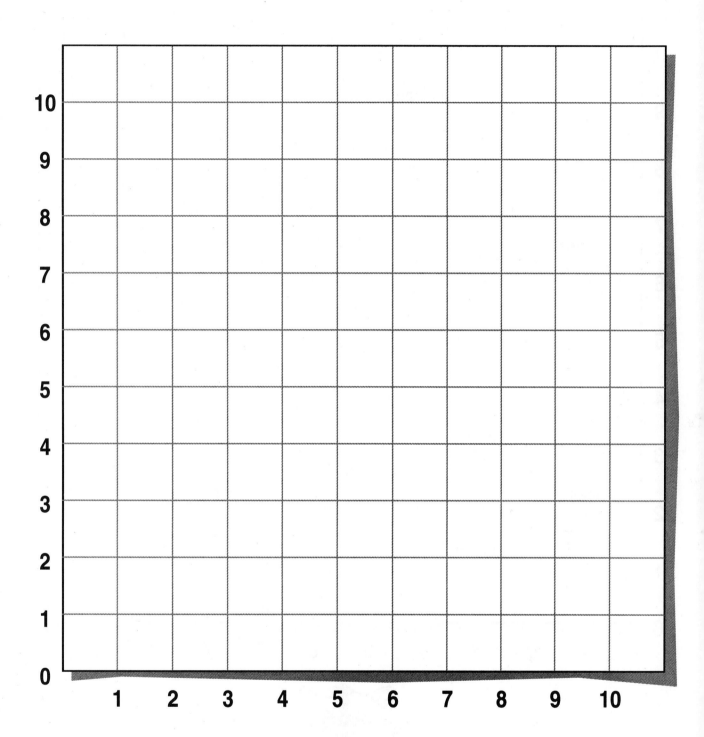

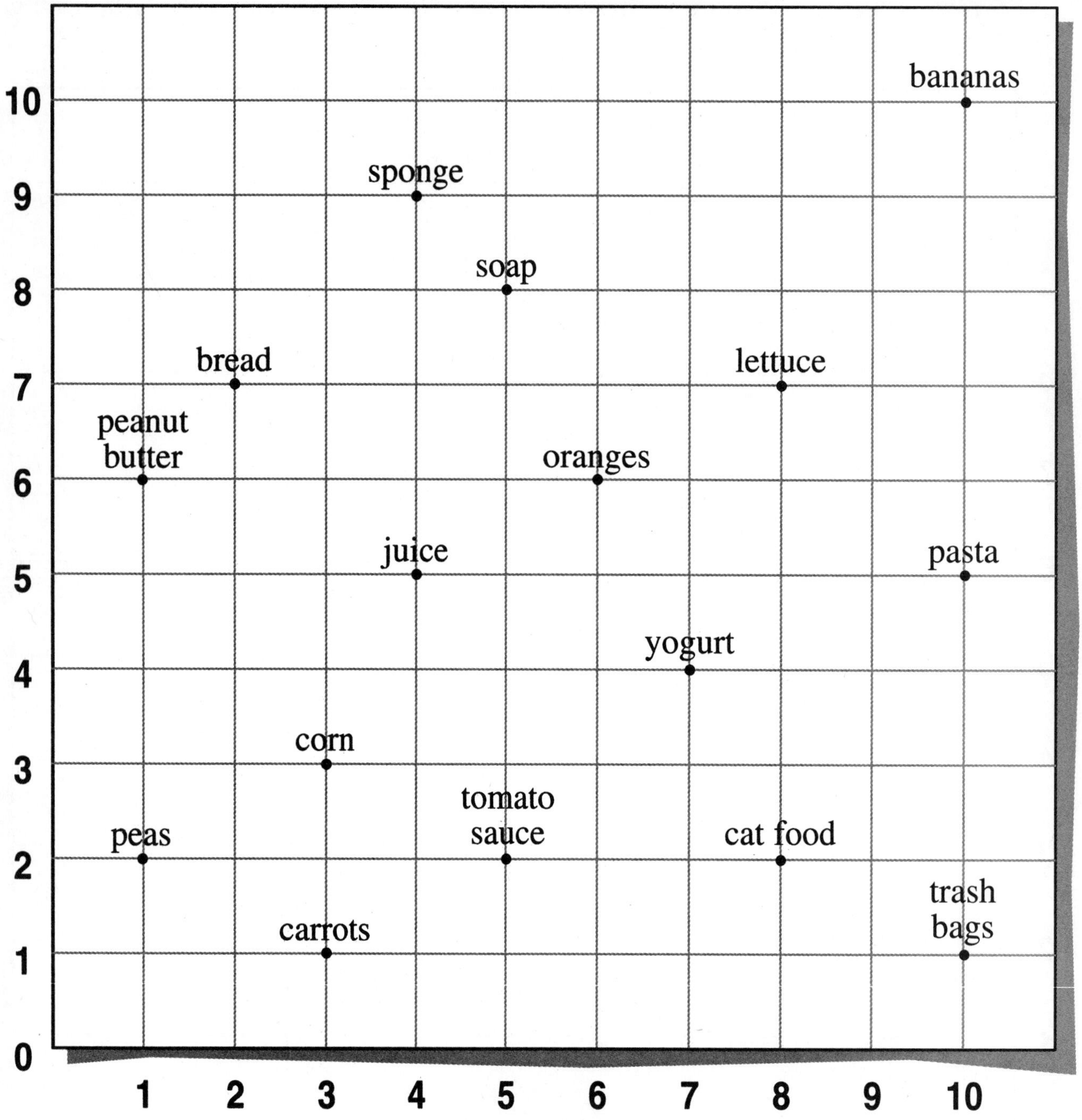
bananas
sponge
soap
bread
lettuce
peanut butter
oranges
juice
pasta
yogurt
corn
tomato sauce
peas
cat food
trash bags
carrots
10
9
8
7
6
5
4
3
2
1
0
1 2 3 4 5 6 7 8 9 10

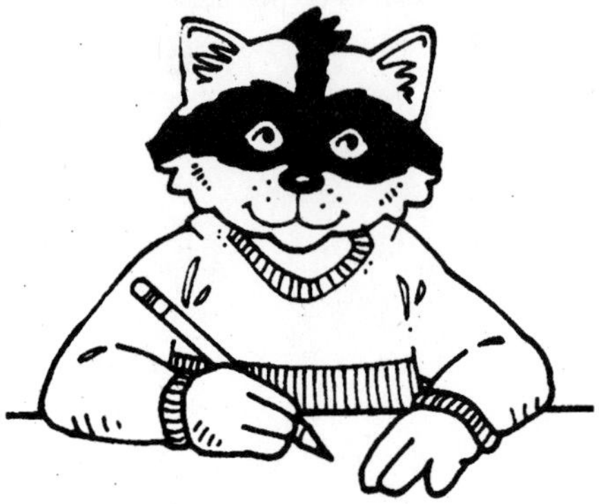

To the teacher: To use this example, have students use ordered pairs to tell what they would buy at the store, or provide ordered pairs to have students find out what to buy.

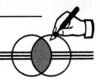

Say Cheese!

Directions Draw a point for each ordered pair. Label each point with a letter name.

	Ordered Pair	Letter Label
1.	(2, 14)	E
2.	(0, 12)	F
3.	(8, 0)	I
4.	(1, 8)	M
5.	(8, 14)	L
6.	(0, 2)	G
7.	(2, 0)	H
8.	(9, 8)	S
9.	(10, 2)	J
10.	(10, 12)	K
11.	(5, 3)	P
12.	(8, 6)	R
13.	(2, 6)	N
14.	(3, 4)	O
15.	(7, 4)	Q

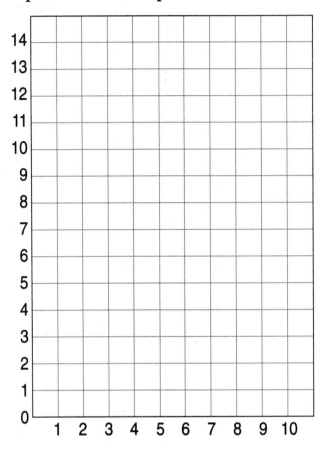

Directions Use your ordered pairs to answer this riddle: **What is the longest word**?

16. Connect **E** to **F** to **G** to **H** to **I** to **J** to **K** to **L** to **E**.

17. Connect **M** to **N** to **O** to **P** to **Q** to **R** to **S**.

18. What is your guess? _____

19. Check your answer by writing the letters for these ordered pairs.

_____ _____ _____ _____ _____ _____,

(9, 8)   (1, 8)   (8, 0)   (8, 14)   (2, 14)   (9, 8)

because there is a mile between the first and last letters.

20. Finish drawing the face on your graph.

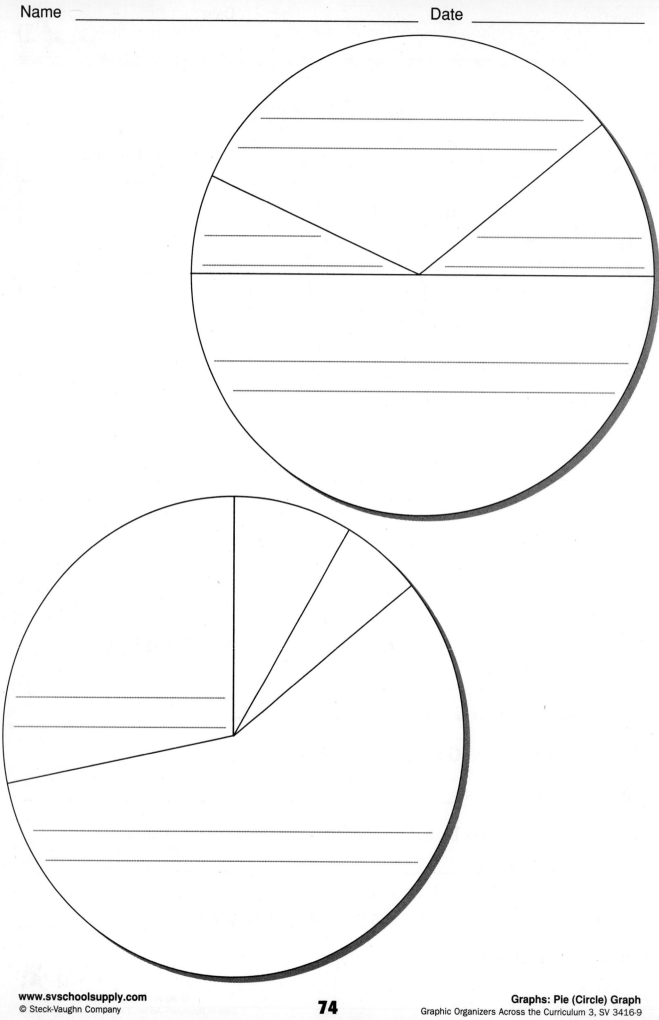

Where We Are From

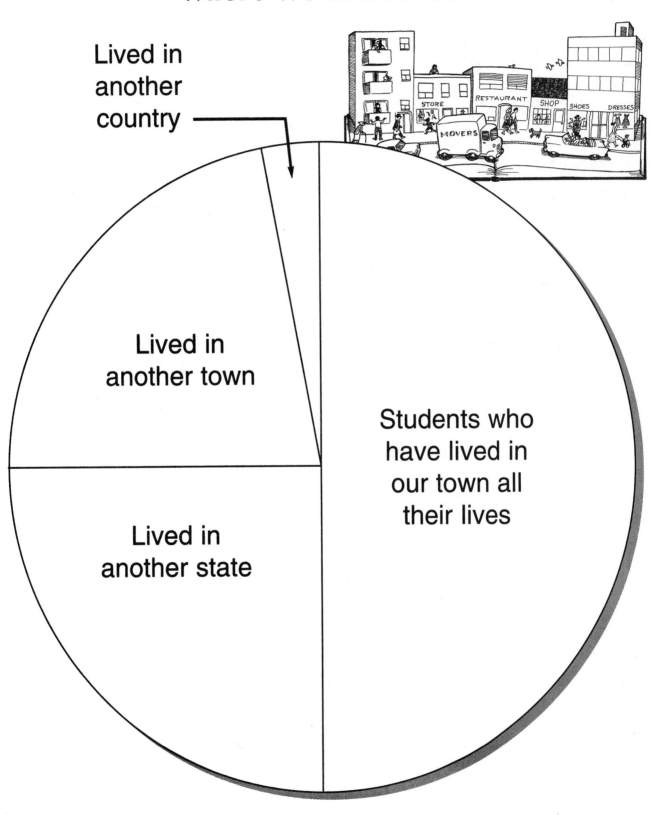

Lived in another country

Lived in another town

Lived in another state

Students who have lived in our town all their lives

Graphs: Pie (Circle) Graph
Graphic Organizers Across the Curriculum 3, SV 3416-9

This Pie's Not for Dessert!

A **pie graph**, or circle graph, divides up a total amount into parts. The parts show clearly which amounts are greater and which are smaller.

Directions Use the information to complete the pie graph. Then, use the graph to answer the questions.

Flower Shop Bulb Sales

1. About half of the bulbs sold were tulip bulbs.

2. Daffodil and crocus bulbs sold in about equal amounts.

3. The number of iris bulbs sold was about the same amount as the daffodil and crocus bulbs together.

4. Assorted other types of bulbs made up the rest of the sales.

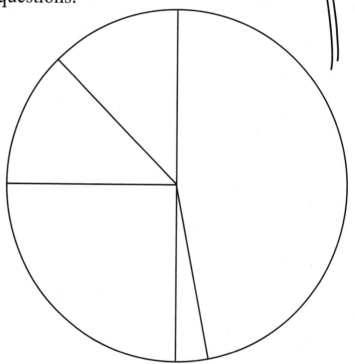

1. Which kind of bulb was the most popular? _____

How do you know? _____

2. People bought 2 kinds of bulbs in about equal amounts. What kinds were they? _____

How do you know? _____

3. Which kind of bulb was the second most popular? _____

How do you know? _____

4. Why do you think this graph is called a pie graph? _____

_____

Name _____   Date _____

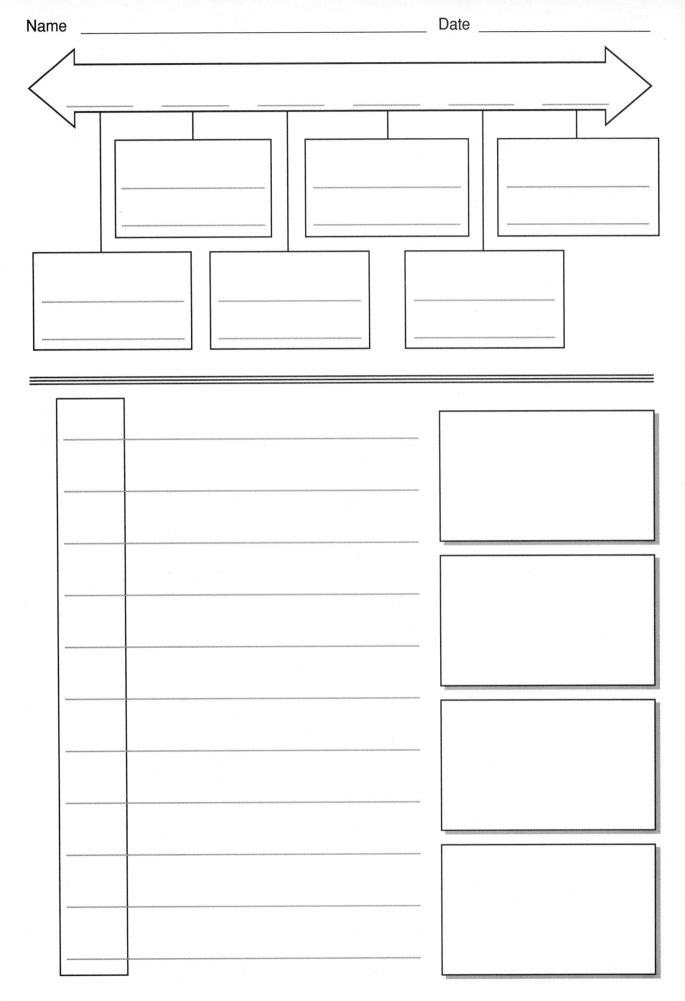

Important Dates in Maine History

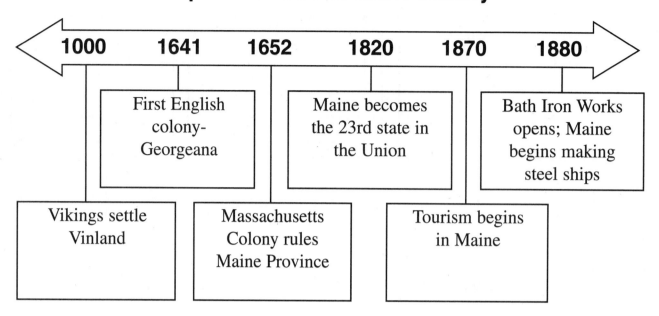

1000	1641	1652	1820	1870	1880

First English colony- Georgeana

Maine becomes the 23rd state in the Union

Bath Iron Works opens; Maine begins making steel ships

Vikings settle Vinland

Massachusetts Colony rules Maine Province

Tourism begins in Maine

Some National Holidays

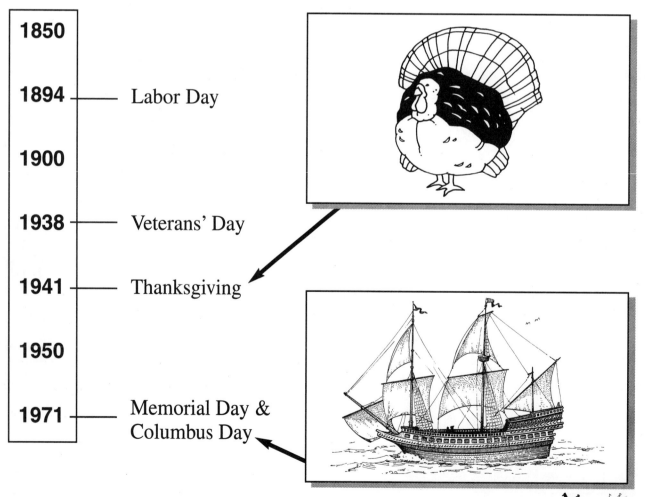

1850	
1894	Labor Day
1900	
1938	Veterans' Day
1941	Thanksgiving
1950	
1971	Memorial Day & Columbus Day

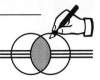

It's in the Mail!

Directions Read the story. Use the blank time line on page 77 to make your own time line. Mark the time line to show when each event happened.

Keeping in touch with loved ones was hard for early settlers in the United States. In the early 1600s, people left letters at inns in seaports and hoped someone would take them to Europe. Between 1672 and 1763, governors in the colonies began planning mail routes. In 1789, the *Constitution* made the post office offical.

That was fine for people who lived in the colonies. Private mail carriers served the settlers who moved west in the mid-1800s. One carrier was the Pony Express. By 1869, the railroad stretched across the country.

As the United States became more settled, the postal service grew. In 1963, a big change came to the whole country. Every address got a ZIP code. ZIP codes made it possible to begin using machines to sort mail.

In recent times, mail delivery has changed most of all. Electronics are the reason for the change. By the early 1990s, people had begun to use fax machines and e-mail for instant communication. What do you think will happen in the future?

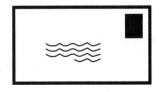

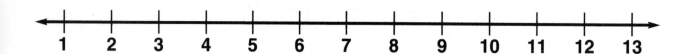

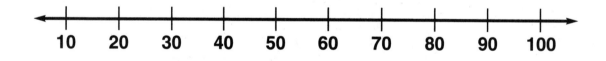

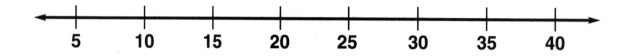

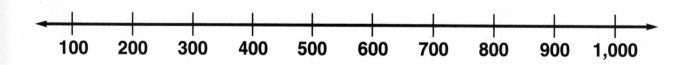

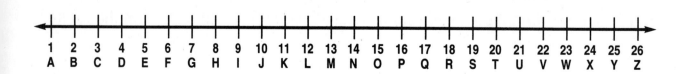

Hop, Skip, and a Jump

Directions Use a number line to find the answer to a multiplication sentence. Make same-size jumps.

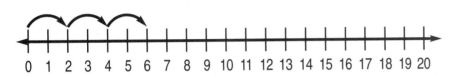

How much are 3 twos?
Take 3 "2-jumps."

$2 + 2 + 2 = 6$

3 twos = 6

$3 \times 2 = 6$

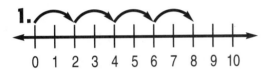

1.

$2 + 2 + 2 + 2 =$ _____

4 twos = _____

$4 \times 2 =$ _____

2.

$3 + 3 + 3 =$ _____

3 threes = _____

$3 \times 3 =$ _____

3.

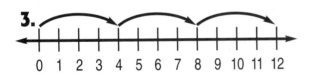

$4 + 4 + 4 =$ _____

3 fours = _____

$3 \times 4 =$ _____

4.

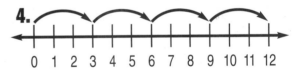

$3 + 3 + 3 + 3 =$ _____

4 threes = _____

$4 \times 3 =$ _____

5.

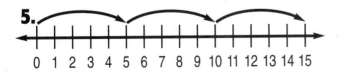

$5 + 5 + 5 =$ _____

3 fives = _____

$3 \times 5 =$ _____

6.

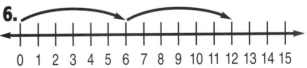

$6 + 6 =$ _____

2 sixes = _____

$2 \times 6 =$ _____

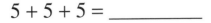

The United States

Map Key
⊛ National capital

Gulf of

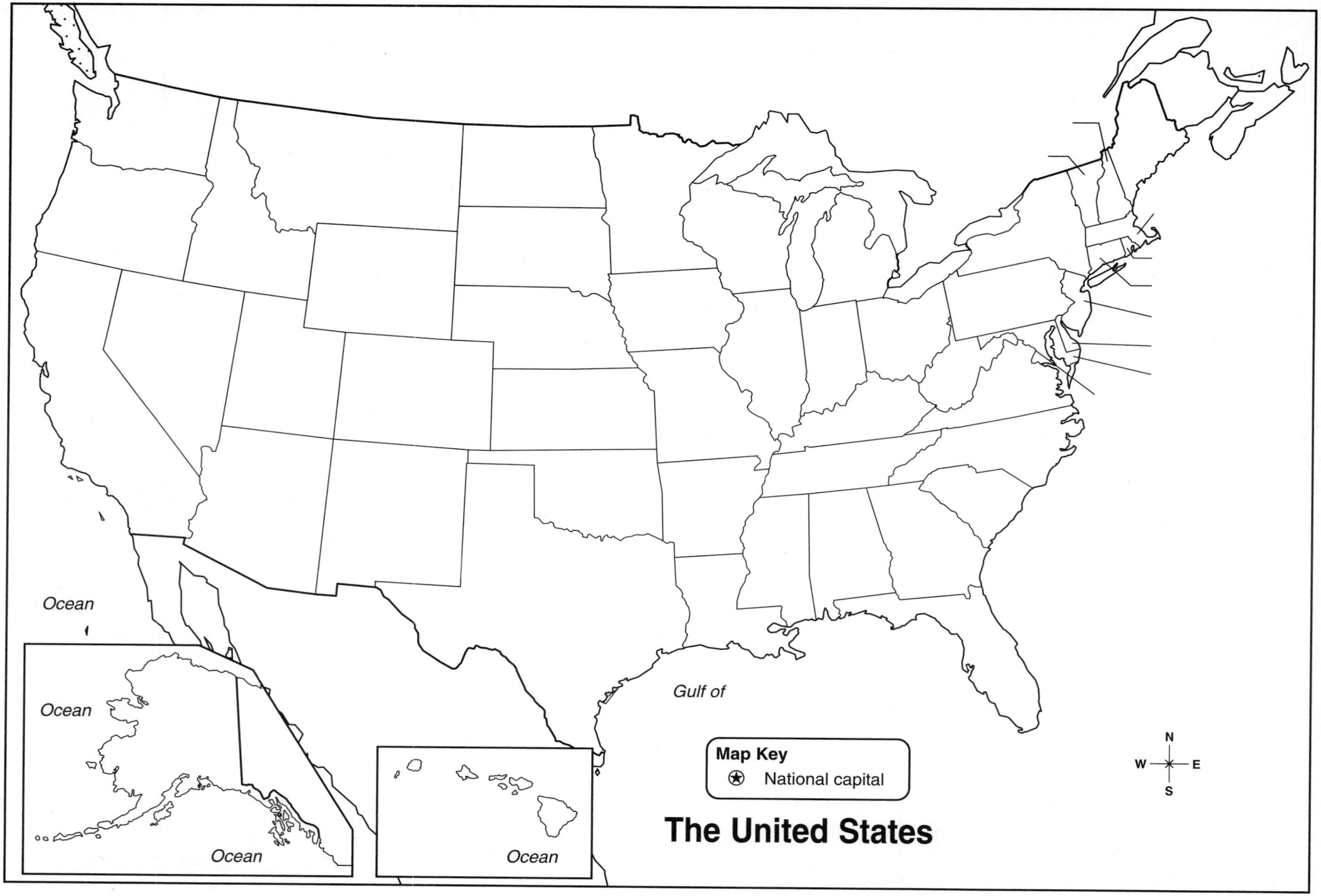

Ocean

Ocean

Ocean

Ocean

N
W — E
S

The United States

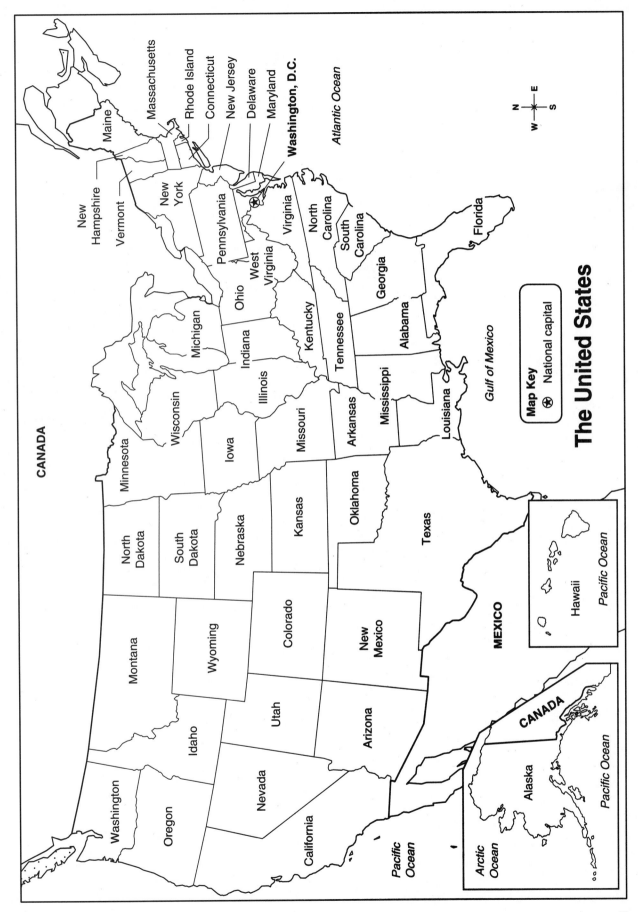

Map Key
⊛ National capital

CANADA

Maine
New Hampshire
Vermont
Massachusetts
Rhode Island
Connecticut
New York
New Jersey
Delaware
Maryland
Washington, D.C.
Pennsylvania
West Virginia
Virginia
North Carolina
South Carolina
Ohio
Kentucky
Tennessee
Georgia
Alabama
Florida
Atlantic Ocean

Michigan
Wisconsin
Illinois
Indiana
Minnesota
Iowa
Missouri
Arkansas
Mississippi
Louisiana
Gulf of Mexico

North Dakota
South Dakota
Nebraska
Kansas
Oklahoma
Texas

Montana
Wyoming
Colorado
New Mexico

Idaho
Utah
Arizona

Washington
Oregon
Nevada
California
Pacific Ocean

MEXICO

Hawaii
Pacific Ocean

CANADA
Alaska
Arctic Ocean
Pacific Ocean

N E S W

www.svschoolsupply.com
© Steck-Vaughn Company

Maps: United States Map
Graphic Organizers Across the Curriculum 3, SV 3416-9

United States

Governments take care of a country's national parks. These parks are lands set aside for everyone to enjoy. The map below shows some of the parks in the United States and some facts about them.

Directions  Use the map to answer the questions.

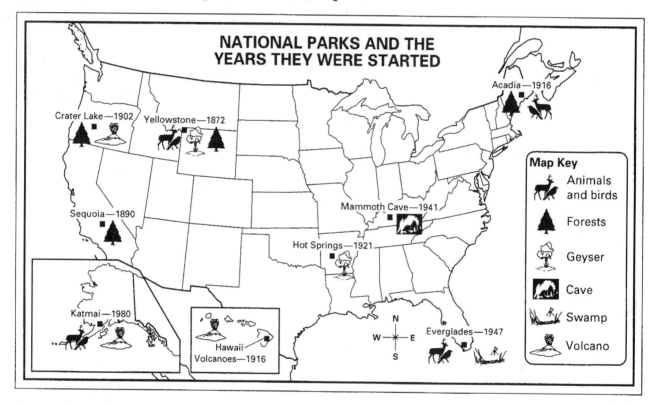

NATIONAL PARKS AND THE YEARS THEY WERE STARTED

Acadia—1916
Crater Lake—1902
Yellowstone—1872
Sequoia—1890
Mammoth Cave—1941
Hot Springs—1921
Katmai—1980
Hawaii Volcanoes—1916
Everglades—1947

Map Key
- Animals and birds
- Forests
- Geyser
- Cave
- Swamp
- Volcano

1. Geysers are springs from which hot water shoots into the air from time to time. What two parks have geysers? Mark each of them with an **X**.

2. Which park shown on the map is the oldest national park?

_____

3. Which park shown on the map is the newest national park? What interesting things could you see there?

_____

4. Circle a park where you would need a light to see things.

THE WORLD

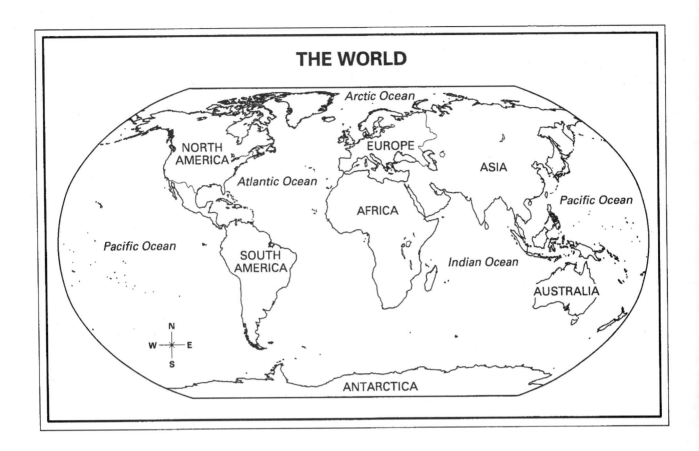

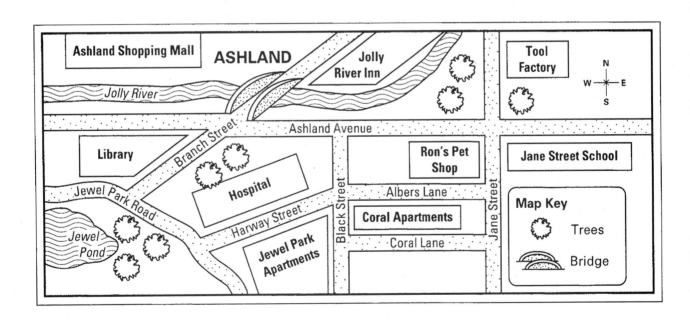

www.svschoolsupply.com
© Steck-Vaughn Company

Maps: World/Neighborhood Maps
Graphic Organizers Across the Curriculum 3, SV 3416-9

Name _____   Date _____

Animals in Danger

Directions This world map shows where some animals live. These animals are in danger. Groups like the World Wildlife Fund want to keep these animals safe. Use the map to answer the questions.

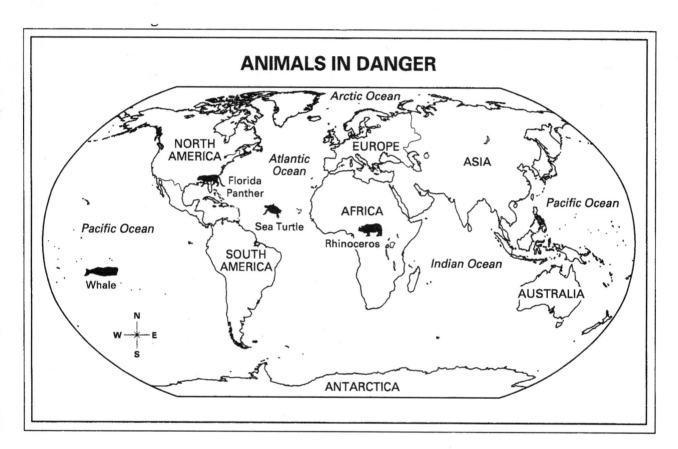

ANIMALS IN DANGER

1. What animal in danger lives in Florida? _____

2. What two animals in danger live in oceans? Circle their names.

   rhinoceros   Florida panther   whale   sea turtle

3. Tigers live in Asia. Put a **T** on the map where tigers live.

4. Grizzly bears live in North America. Put a **B** where they live.

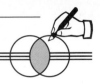

Franklin's Home Town

Directions This map shows the downtown area of Philadelphia in 1787. Use the map to answer the questions.

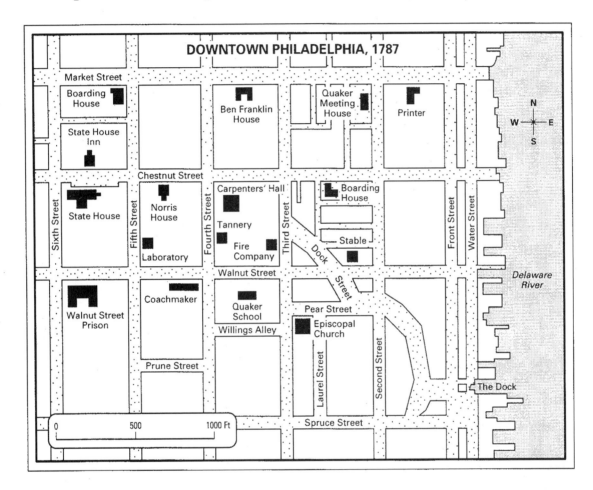

1. About how far would Ben Franklin have to walk from home to the printer?

_____

2. Trace the route you would take from the Episcopal Church to the State House.

3. Circle the building that is farthest east on the map.

4. What direction is Carpenters' Hall from the Quaker School?

_____

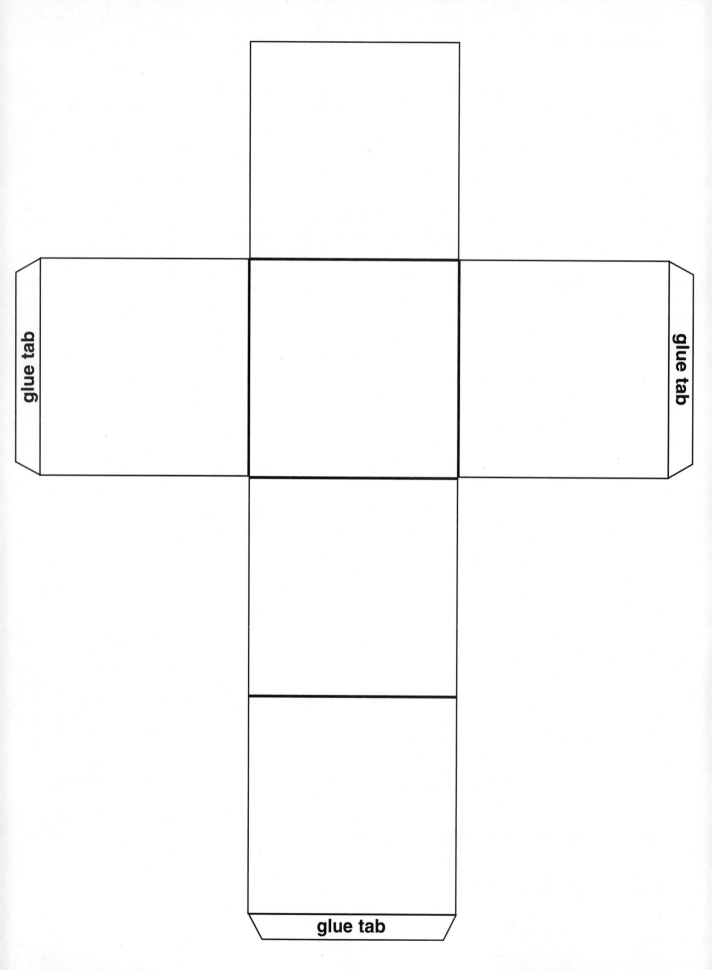

glue tab

glue tab

glue tab

Language & Memory Aids: Cubing
Graphic Organizers Across the Curriculum 3, SV 3416-9

Italy

glue tab

Russia

England

Canada

glue tab

China

France

glue tab

Cube It!

A **cube** can help you to think and write. You can write your ideas about something on each side of the cube. Then, cut out the cube and paste or tape it together. Toss the cube into the air. When it lands, write about the idea that faces up on the cube.

Directions Choose one of these activities. Use the blank cube on page 88 to complete the activity.

Activity 1:

Think about the way people did things many, many years ago. For example, how did they travel? Where did they get their food? On each side of the cube, write one thing that you think has changed. Make and toss your cube. Read the side that faces up. Talk about it. Find out more about it. Then, write about it.

Activity 2:

Think about the different kinds of places where animals can live. Some live where it is cold. Some live in humid rain forests. On each side of the cube, name a kind of place. Make and toss your cube. Read the side that faces up. What kinds of animals live there? Find out. Write about them.

Activity 3:

There are many different types of writing. On your cube, write **news article**, **mystery**, **poetry**, **science fiction**, **historical fiction**, and **humorous**. Make and toss your cube. Read the side that faces up. Write something in that style. You may want to read some samples of that kind of writing before you begin.

WHAT IS THE WORD?
Write the word here.

_____

WHAT DOES THE WORD MEAN?
Write the meaning here.

_____

_____

_____

_____

WHAT DOES THE WORD STAND FOR?
Draw a picture of it here.

HOW CAN YOU USE THE WORD?
Write a sentence using the word here.

_____

_____

_____

_____

WHAT IS THE WORD?
Write the word here.

trouble

WHAT DOES THE WORD MEAN?
Write the meaning here.

Trouble is when you have a problem.

WHAT DOES THE WORD STAND FOR?
Draw a picture of it here.

HOW CAN YOU USE THE WORD?
Write a sentence using the word here.

I got into trouble because my room was a big mess.

Language & Memory Aids: Word Cards
Graphic Organizers Across the Curriculum 3, SV 3416-9

Card Clues

Word cards can help you learn and remember new words. On word cards, you write the word. Then, you write the meaning of the word. Then, you draw a picture of the word or what the word means. Last, you use the word in a sentence.

Directions Choose one of these activities about the human body. Use the blank Word Cards on page 91 to complete the activity.

Activity 1:

Your word for this activity is **muscle**. Write **muscle** in the first box. Find out what the word means. Write the meaning in the second box. Draw a picture of what our muscles can do for us in the third box. Then, use the word in a sentence in the last box. Cut out your cards and staple them together in one corner.

Activity 2:

Your word for this activity is **organ**. Write **organ** in the first box. Find out what the word means with regard to the human body. Write the meaning in the second box. Draw a picture of a person with an arrow showing where one of the human organs is in the third box. Then, use the word in a sentence in the last box. Cut out your cards and staple them together in one corner.

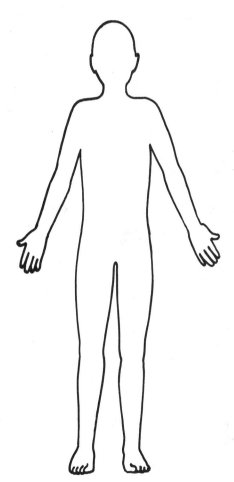

Activity 3:

Your word for this activity is **skeleton**. Write **skeleton** in the first box. Find out what the word means. Write the meaning in the second box. Draw a picture of a skeleton in the third box. Then, use the word in a sentence in the last box. Cut out your cards and staple them together in one corner.

Name _____ Date _____

Graphic Organizers Across the Curriculum
Grade Three

Answer Key

P. 9
Answers will vary.

P. 12
Answers will vary.

P. 15
Answers will vary.

P. 18
1. migrate
2. camouflage
3. bear
4. whale, Canadian goose, monarch butterfly
5. Answers will vary.

P. 21
Answers will vary.

P. 24
Greg: X, yes, X, X
Lisa: yes, X, X, X
Ben: X, X, yes, X
Sara: X, X, X, yes

P. 26
3: 4, 5, 6, 7, 8, 9, 10, 11, 12, 13
4: 5, 6, 7, 8, 9, 10, 11, 12, 13, 14
5: 6, 7, 8, 9, 10, 11, 12, 13, 14, 15
6: 7, 8, 9, 10, 11, 12, 13, 14, 15, 16
7: 8, 9, 10, 11, 12, 13, 14, 15, 16, 17
8: 9, 10, 11, 12, 13, 14, 15, 16, 17, 18
9: 10, 11, 12, 13, 14, 15, 16, 17, 18, 19
10: 11, 12, 13, 14, 15, 16, 17, 18, 19, 20
1. 12
2. 10
3. 14
4. 10
5. 6
6. 8

P. 29
1. 5:00
2. 4:00
3. Channel 2
4. 1 1/2 hours
5. Channel 5
6. Channel 8
7. The Wilsons
8. Pay the Price

P. 30
Homework: 3:30, 4:15, 45 minutes
Play outside: 4:15, 5:15, 1 hour
Read: 5:15, 5:45, 30 minutes
Chores: 5:45, 6:00, 15 minutes
Answers to students' after-school schedules will vary.

P. 33
Topic: Birds
Large circle: Migrating Birds; smaller circles: snow goose, swan
Large circle: Birds that Can't Fly; smaller circles: ostrich, penguin
Large circle: Birds of Prey; smaller circles: eagle, owl
Large circle: Water Birds; smaller circles; duck, swan

P. 36
Characters: Kenny, Grandpa
Setting: Kenny's house and yard
Problem: Grandpa hurts his ankle.
Events: Family eats Thanksgiving dinner; family leaves; Kenny and Grandpa pass a football; Grandpa steps in a hole and hurts his ankle.
Solution: Kenny calls for help, and an ambulance arrives.

P. 37
Character: Dreamer/poet
Setting: Bed
Problem: There are too many things to count.
Events: Dreamer dreams there are many, many things to see. Dreamer hears a voice saying to count everything. Dreamer tries to count, but there are too many things.
Solution: Dreamer wakes up and remembers there is a math test.

P. 40
Rain: yes, no, no
Stove: no, yes, yes
Computer screen: no, no, yes
Star: yes, yes, yes
Fire: no, yes, yes
Radiator: no, yes, no
Your body: no, yes, no
Cloud: yes, no, no
Light bulb: no, no, yes
Sun: yes, yes, yes
Flashlight: no, no, yes
Lightning: yes, no, yes
Yes. A & B.
Venn diagram:
In A: rain, cloud
In B: your body, radiator
In C: computer screen, light bulb, flashlight
In A&B: None
In A&C: lightning
In B&C: fire, stove
In A, B, & C: Sun, star

P. 43
Possible answers:
1. Group: Math operations
   Description: Addition: adding numbers together to get a sum; Subtraction: subtracting numbers to get a difference; Multiplication: multiplying numbers to get a product; Division: Dividing numbers to get a quotient.
   Examples will vary.
2. Group: Animals
   Description: Mammal: animal with fur, warm blooded, has live young; Reptile: cold blooded, lays eggs; Fish: cold blooded, has gills, lays eggs; Bird: warm blooded, has wings, lays egg with shell.
   Possible examples: Mammal: dog, monkey, bear; Reptile: lizard, snake; Fish: salmon, shark; Bird: robin, eagle

P. 46
Answers will vary.

P. 48
1. Cause: The weather was bad.; Effect: School was cancelled.
2. Cause: Scott and Joey stopped to play on the way to the bus stop.; Effect: The bus left without them.
3. Cause: It was Julie's birthday.; Effect: There was a big party for her.
4. Cause: Juan waited a long time for a puppy.; Effect: He was very happy when his mother brought one home.
5. Cause: Nina did not eat breakfast.; Effect: She felt hungry.

P. 51
1. Cause: You eay a healthy diet.; Effects: You will feel better. You will look better. You will have more energy.
2. Causes: The electricity was out. The telephone wire was broken. There was water over the road.; Effect: Jeremy could not get in touch with his family.

P. 54
Maps will vary. Check students' work.

P. 57
Activity 1: Stages are: Egg, Caterpillar, Chrysalis, Butterfly. Check pictures for accuracy and understanding.
Activity 2: Stages are: New Moon, Half Moon, Full Moon, Half Moon. Check pictures for accuracy and understanding.

P. 60
1. $30,000, $25,000
2. 1985, $35,000
3. 1980
4. $5,000

P. 61
Surveys and graphs will vary. Check students' work.

P. 64
1. $2
2. $5
3. Football
4. Soccer
5. Basketball and Skating
6. $3
7. Check students' graphs.
8. $1

P. 65
Surveys and graphs will vary. Check students' work.

P. 68
1. Bear Sightings
2. 2 bears
3. 12 bears
4. Thursday
5. Graphs and questions will vary.

P. 70
Check students' graphs.

P. 73
1–17. Students graphs look roughly like a face with a smile.
18. Answers will vary.
19. S, M, I, L, E, S
20. Students can draw eyes, nose, ears, hair, etc.

P. 76
Beginning at largest part of graph and going clockwise: tulip bulbs, other bulbs, iris bulbs, crocus or daffodil bulbs, crocus or daffodil bulbs.
1. Tulip bulbs; because they take up more of the pie chart than any other kind.
2. Daffodil and crocus bulbs; because their sections of the pie graph are the same size.
3. Iris bulbs; because they take up the second largest part of the graph.
4. Answers will vary.

P. 79
Times lines will vary. Check students' work.

P. 81
1. 8, 8, 8
2. 9, 9, 9
3. 12, 12, 12
4. 12, 12, 12
5. 15, 15, 15
6. 12, 12, 12

P. 84
1. Yellowstone and Hot Springs should be marked with an **X**.
2. Yellowstone
3. Katmai; volcano, animals and birds
4. Mammoth Cave should be circled.

P. 86
1. Florida Panther
2. whale, sea turtle
3. Students put a "T" on Asia.
4. Students put a "B" on North America.

P. 87
1. About 1,000 feet.
2. Check students' maps. Possible route: North on Third Street to Walnut Street. West on Walnut Street to Sixth Street. North on Sixth Street to the State House.
3. Printer should be circled.
4. North

P. 90
Answers will vary.

P. 93
1. Word: Muscle; Definition: parts of the body that expand and contract to cause the body to move; Pictures and sentences will vary.
2. Word: Organ; Definition: a group of tissues dedicated to a specific purpose in the body; Pictures and sentences will vary.
3. Word: Skeleton; Definition: the hard framework of a body; Pictures and sentences will vary.